STRESS RELIEVING PATTERNS

MYSTICAL CIRCLE

COLORING BOOK FOR ADULTS

Vol.2

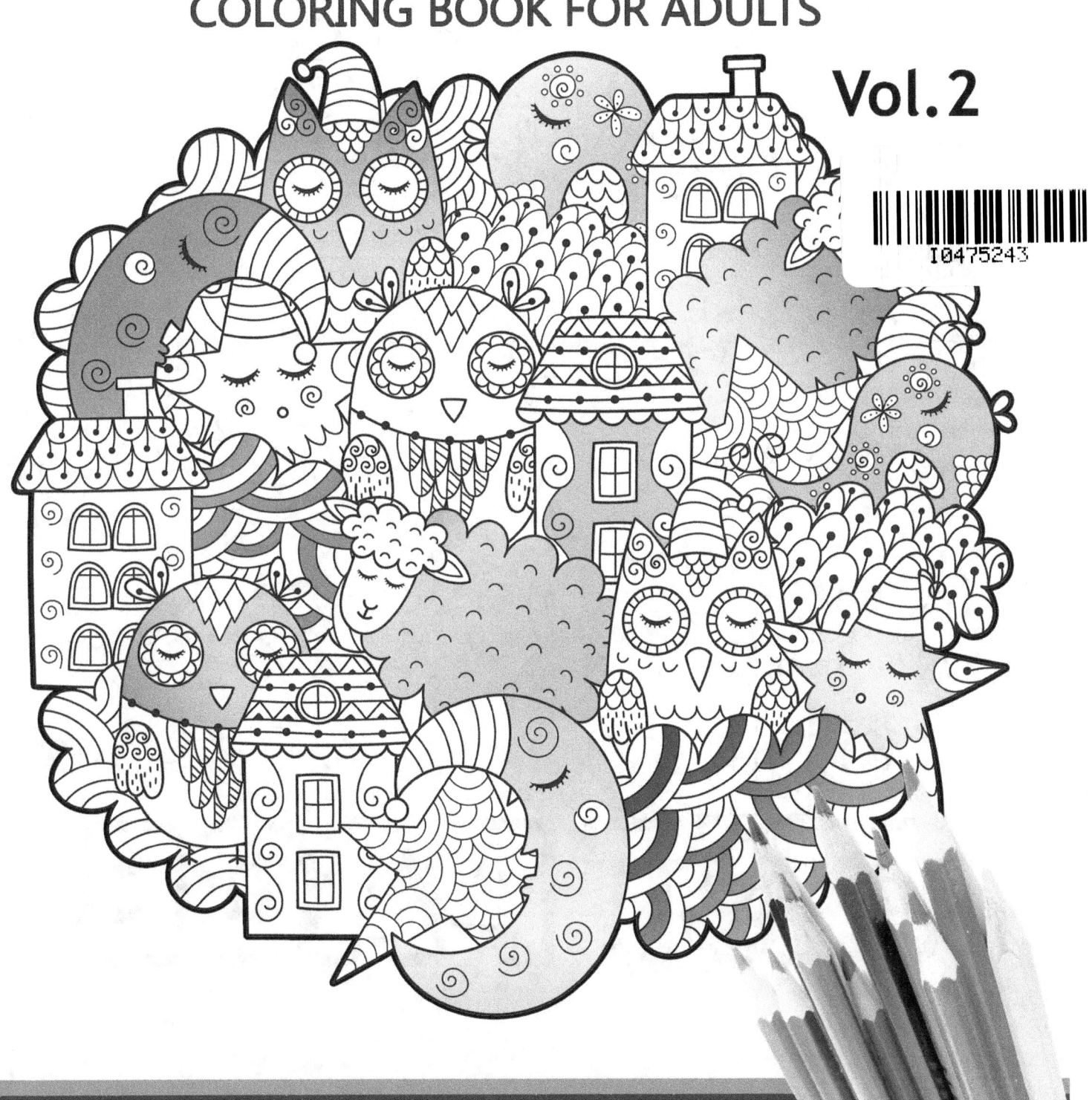

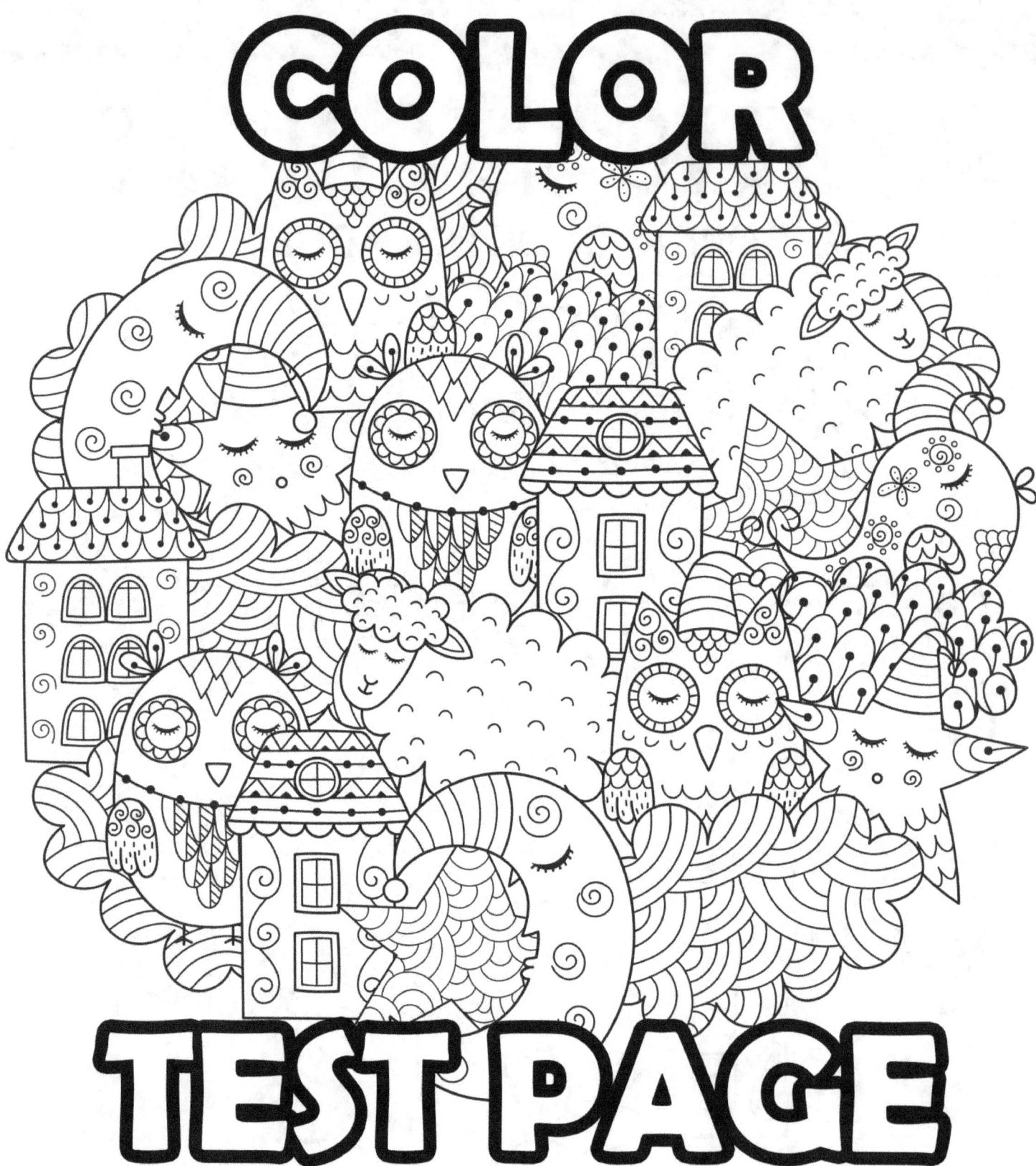

TEST YOUR COLOR

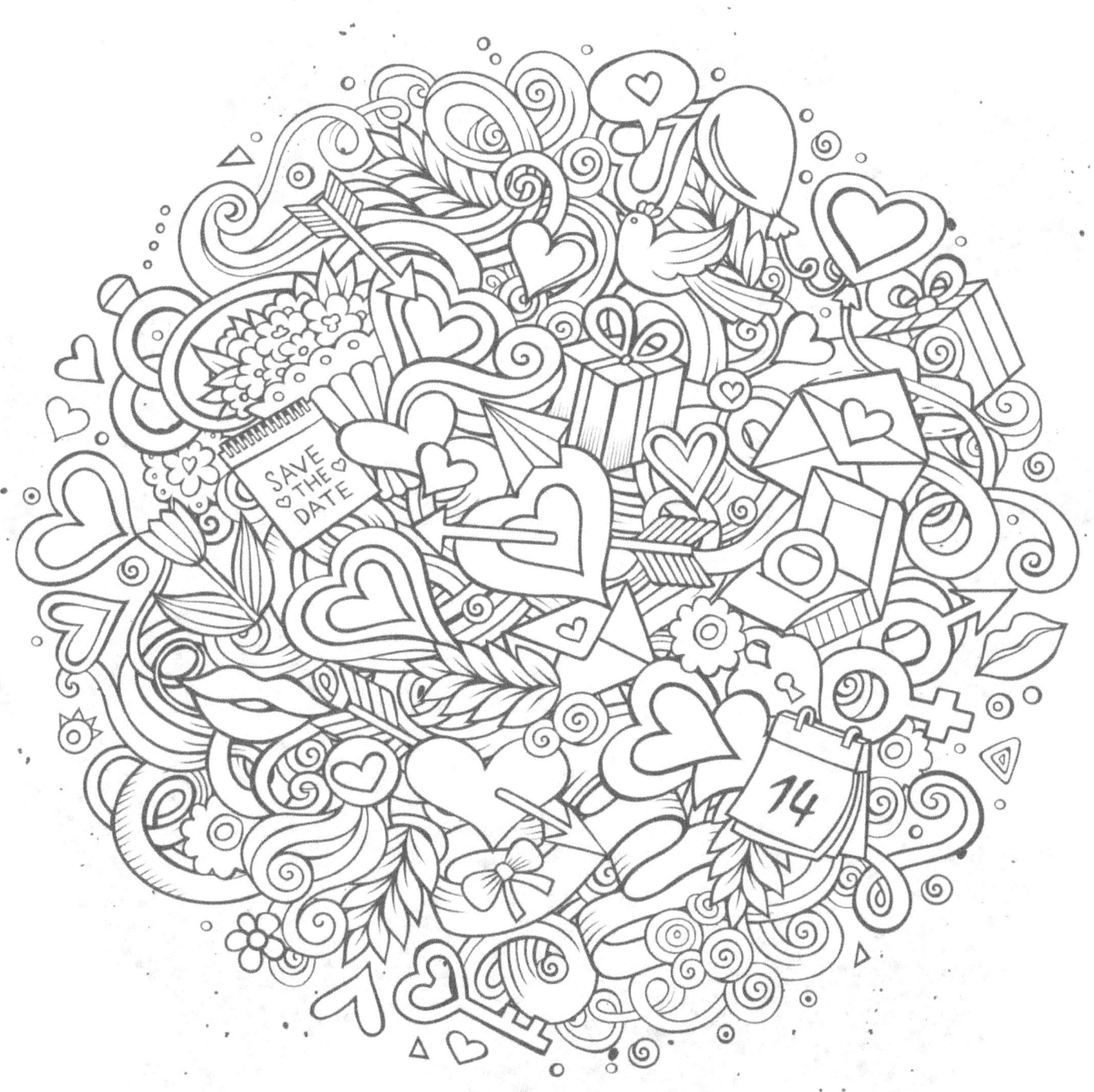

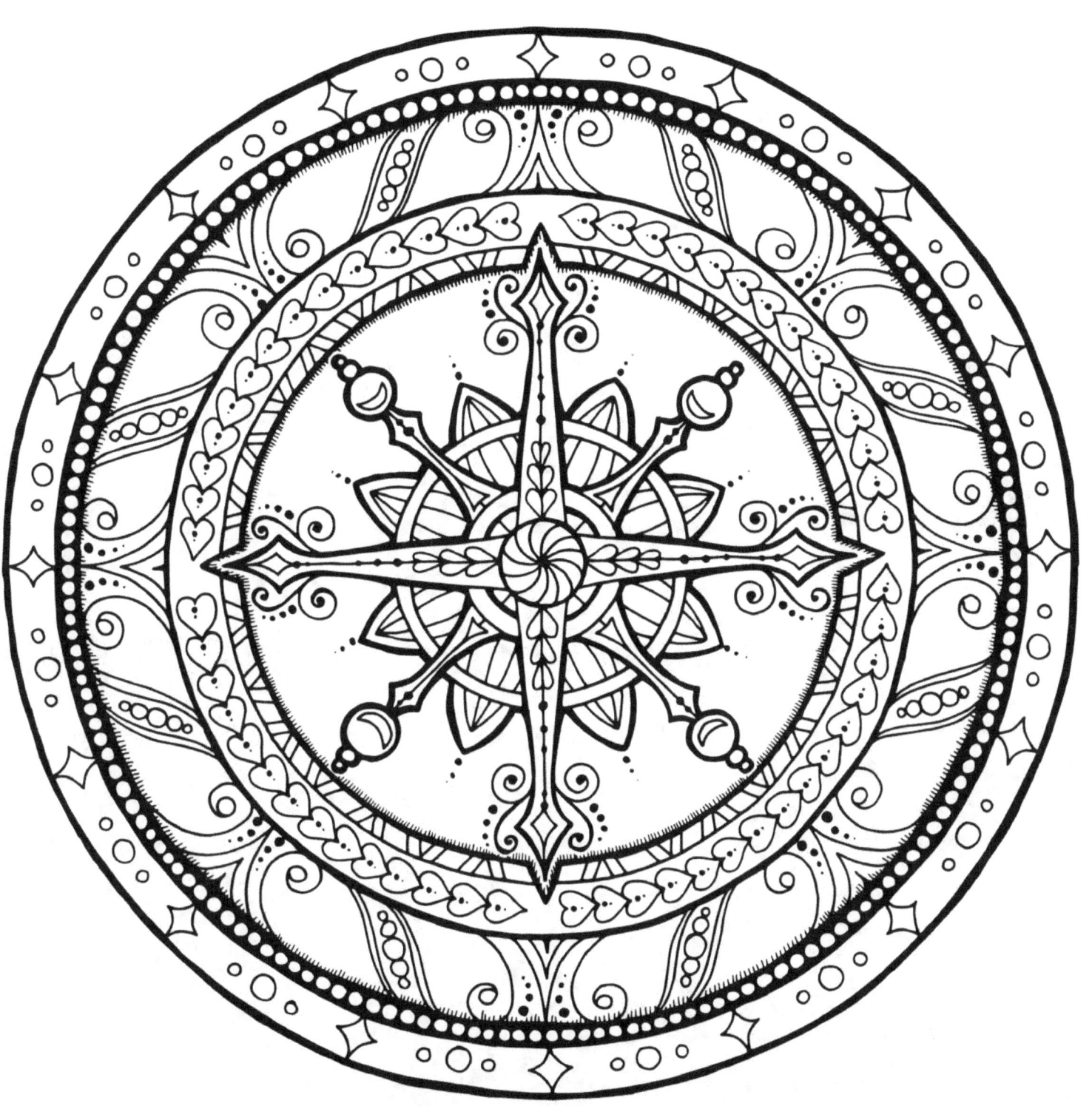

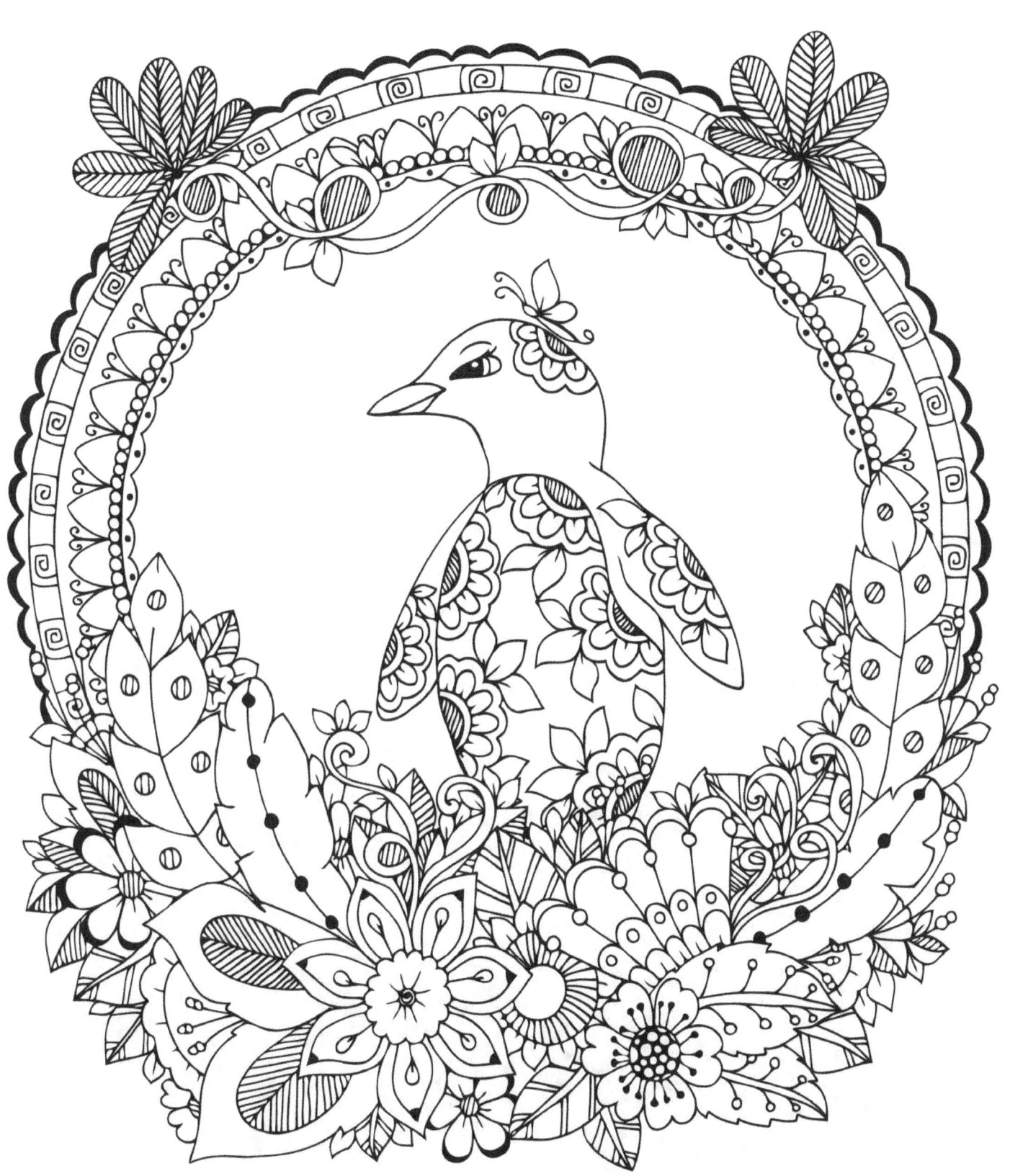

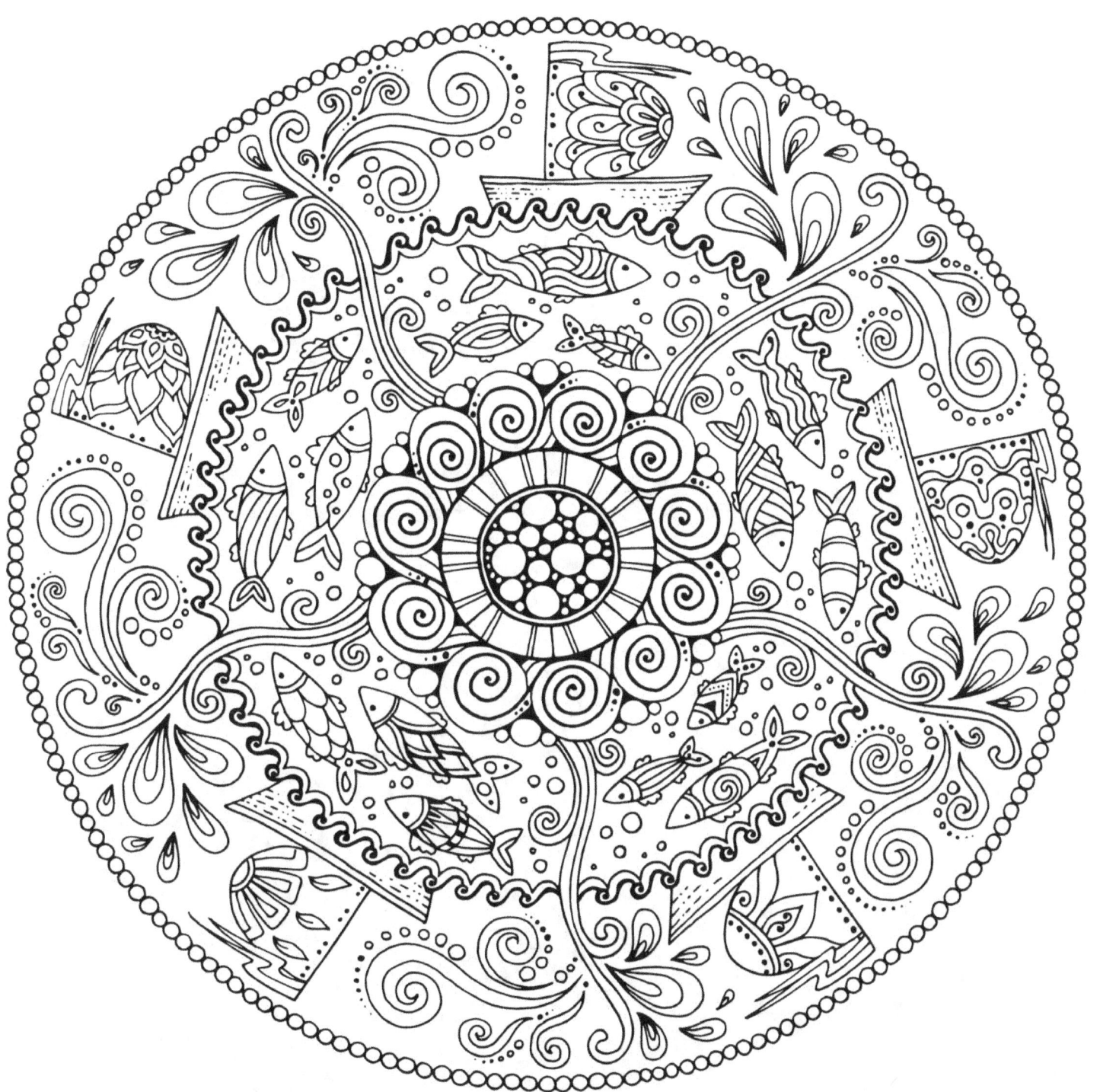

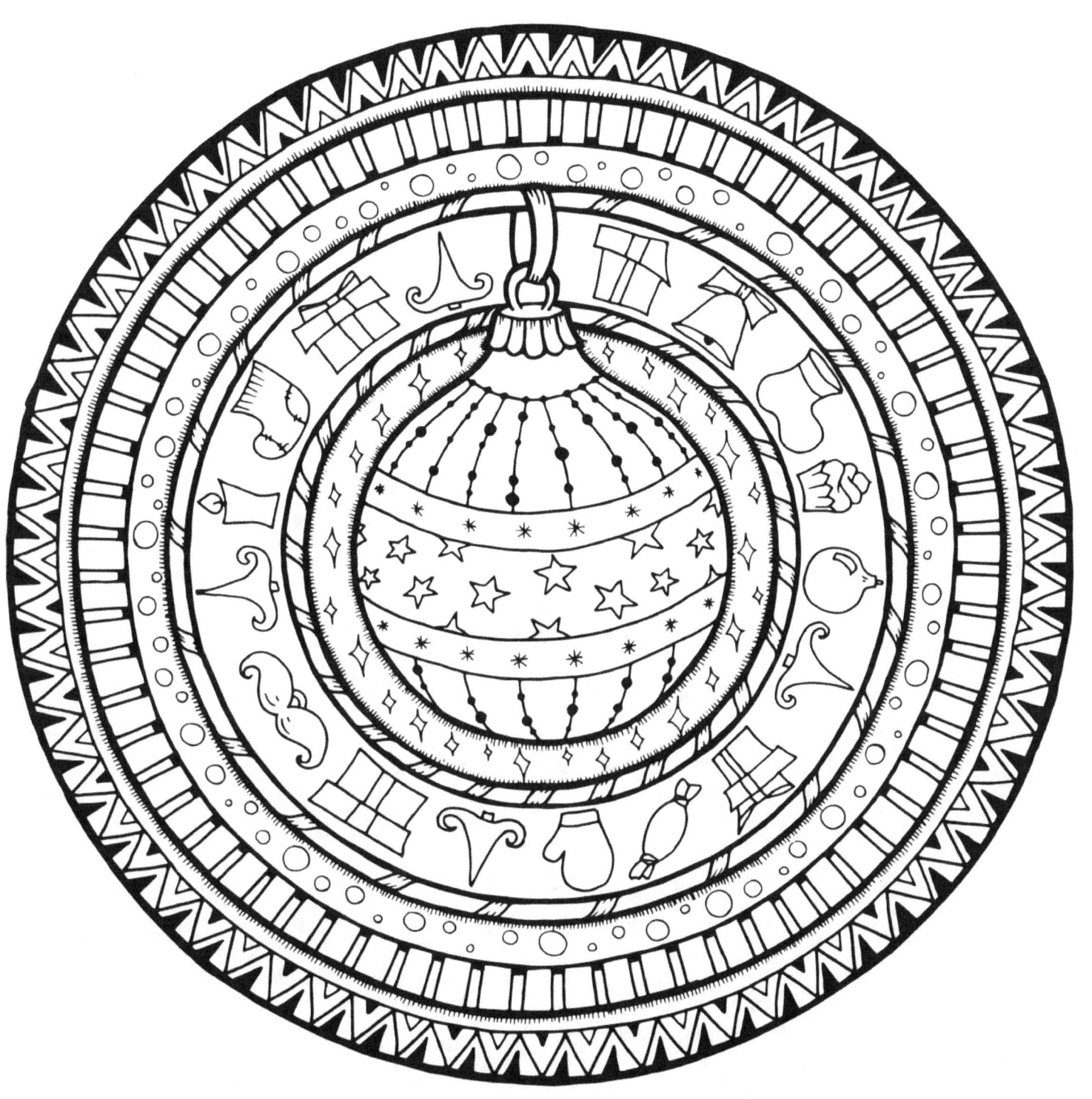

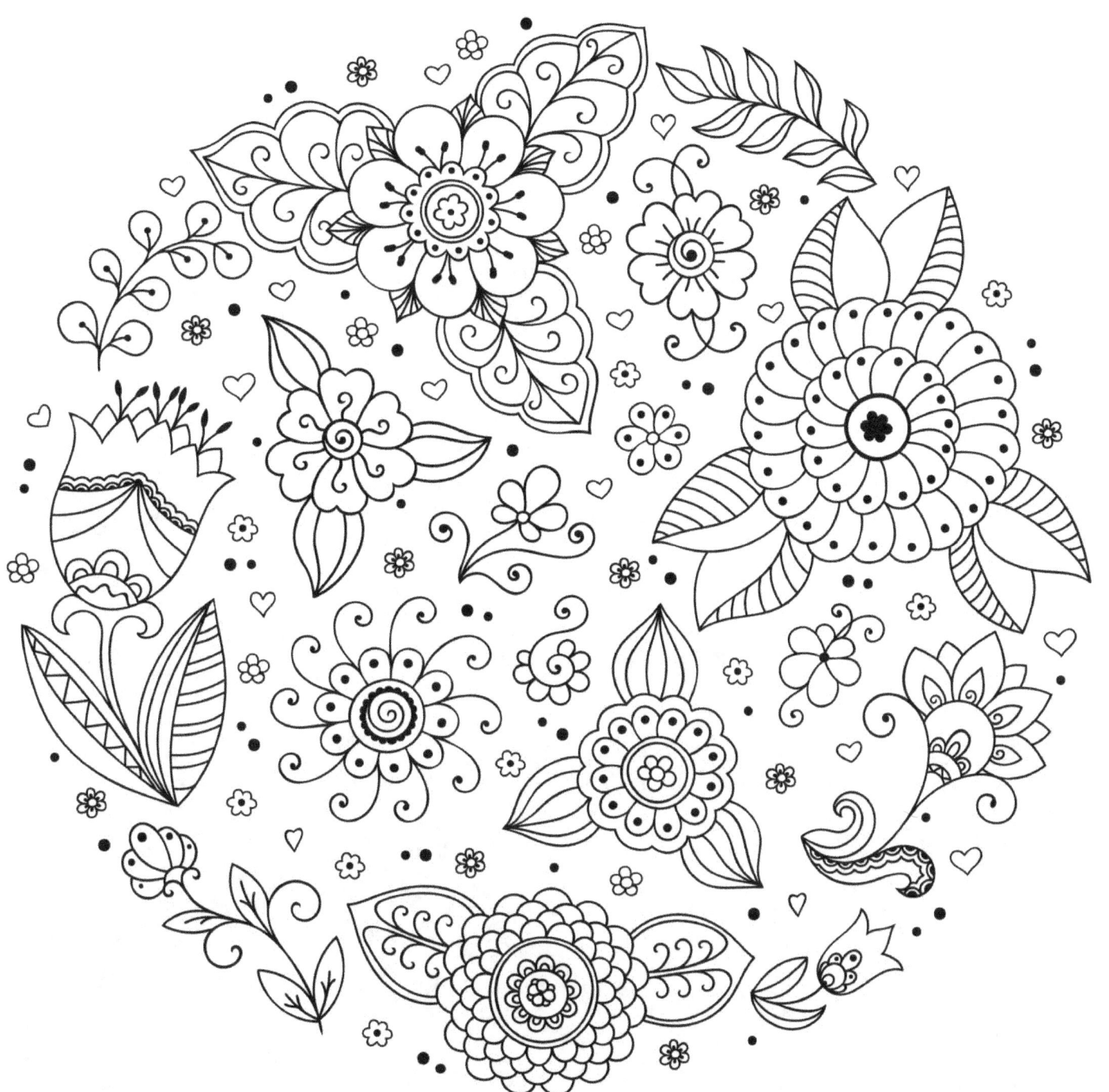

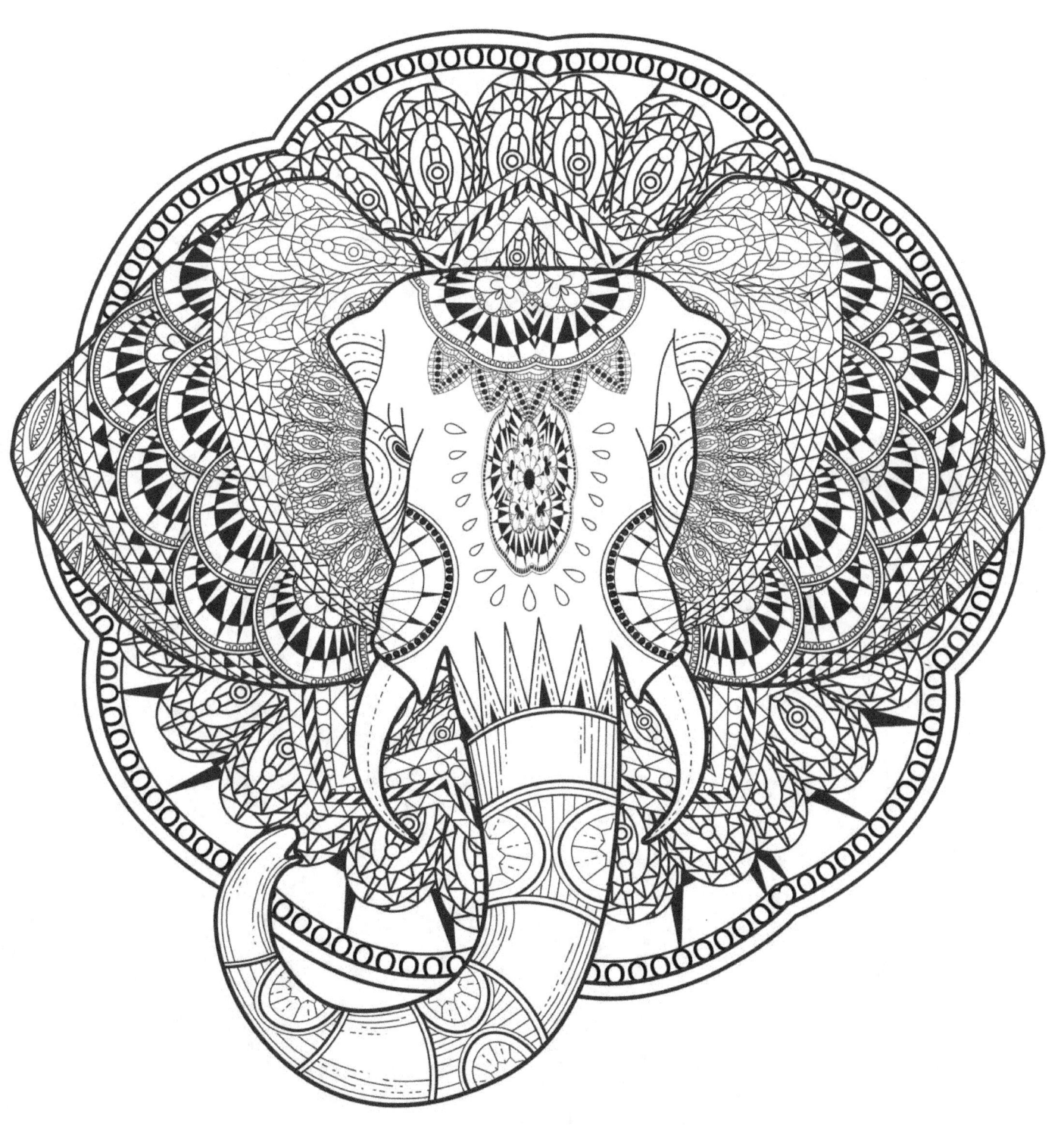

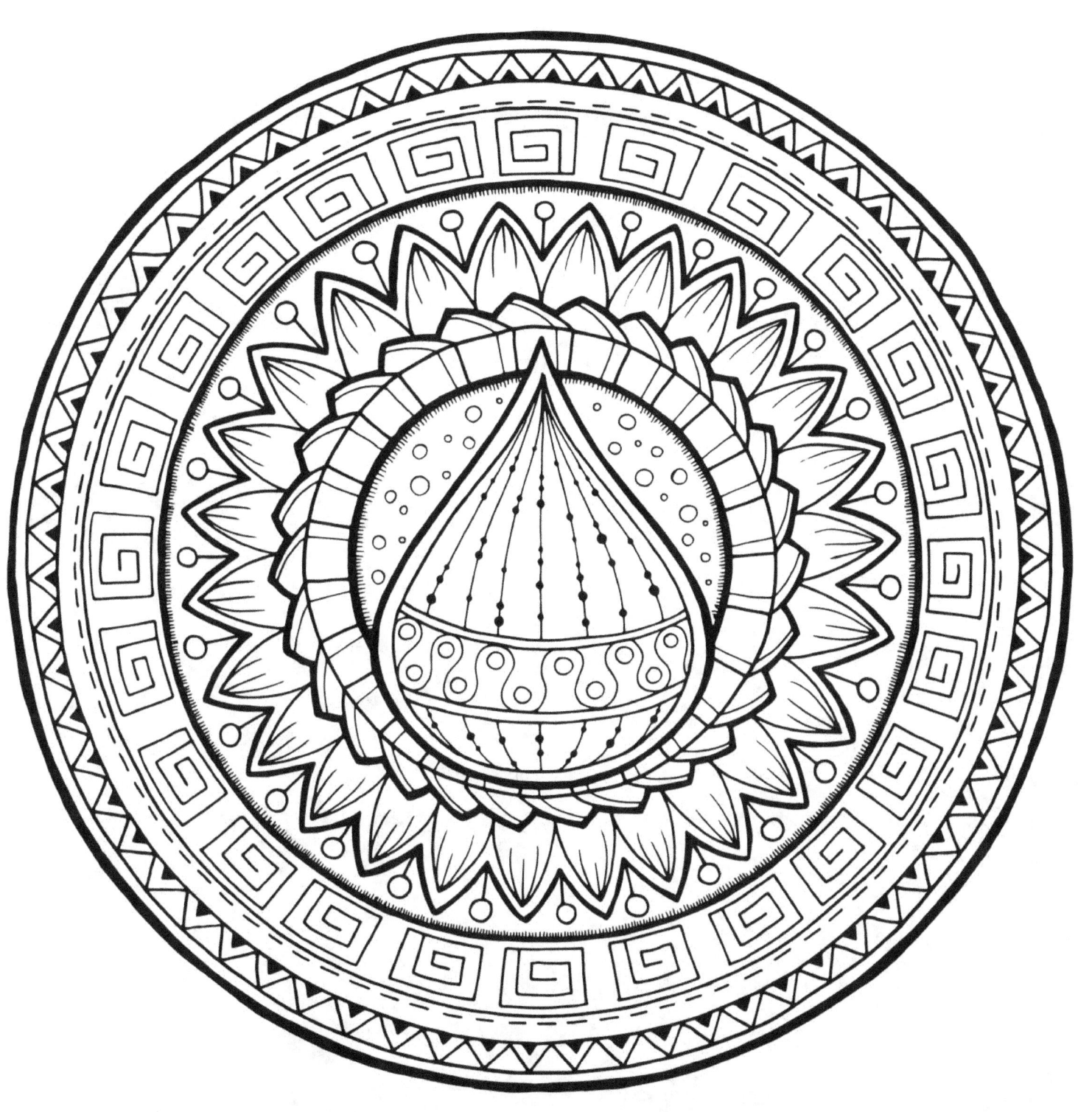

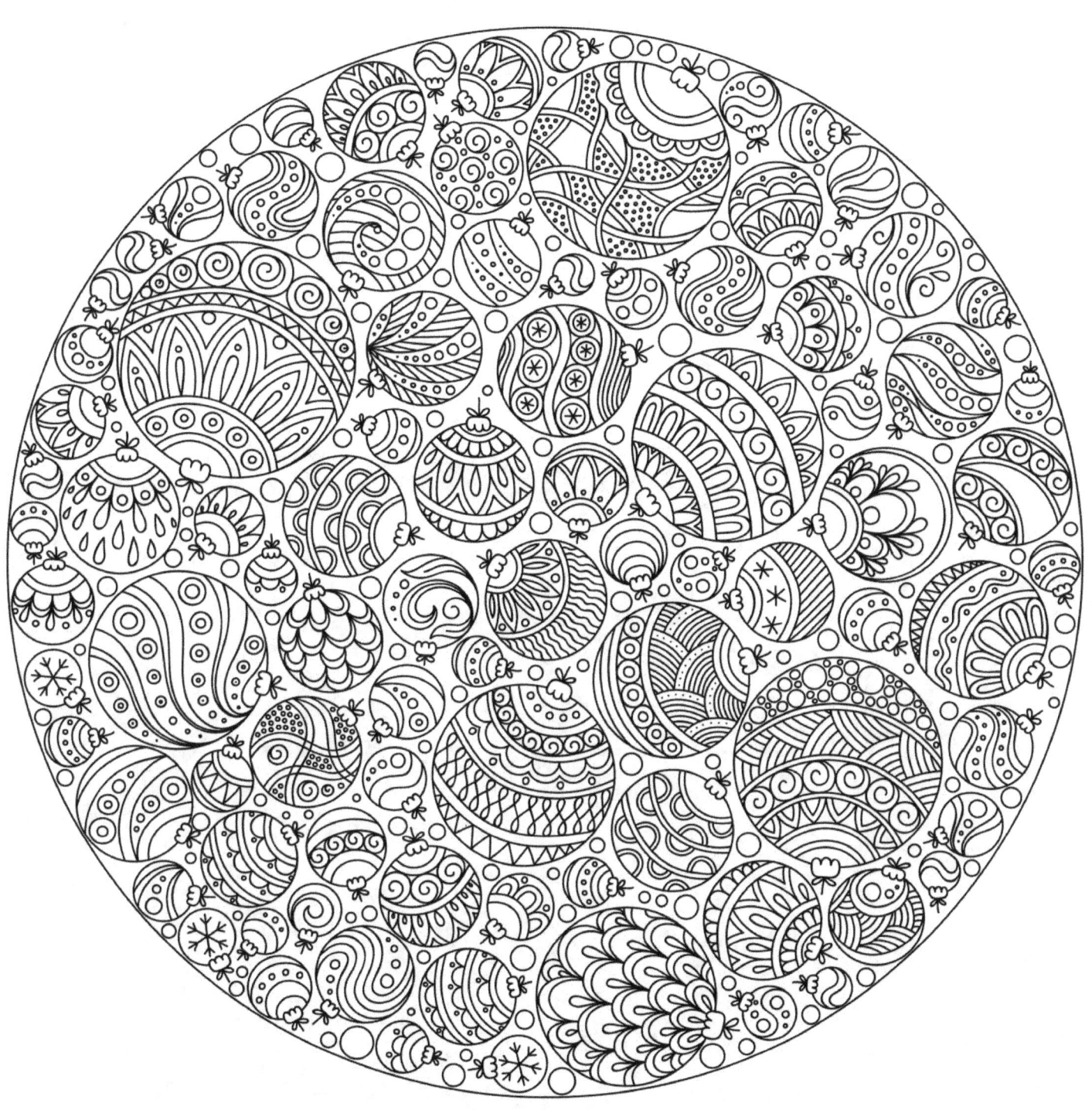

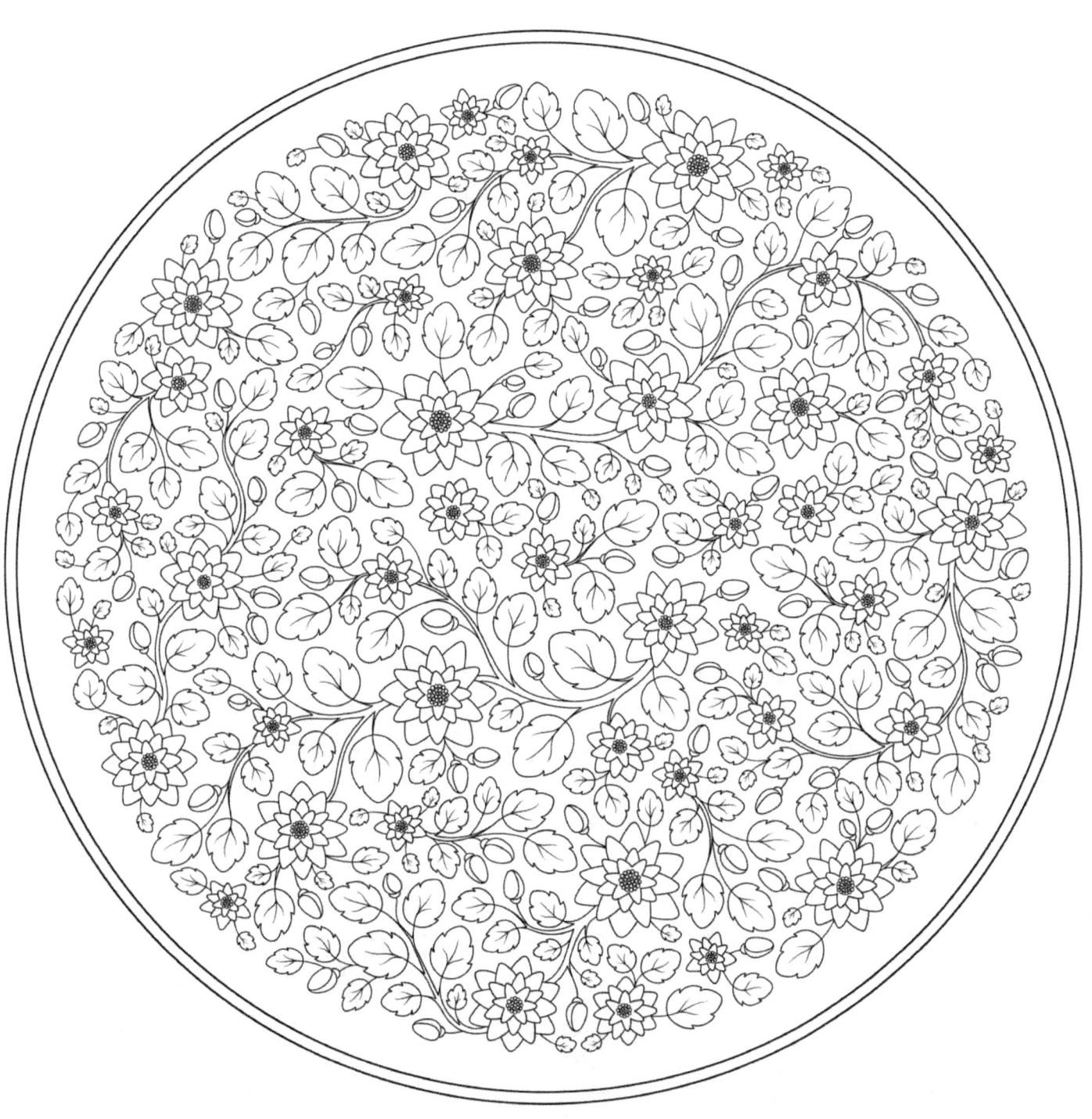

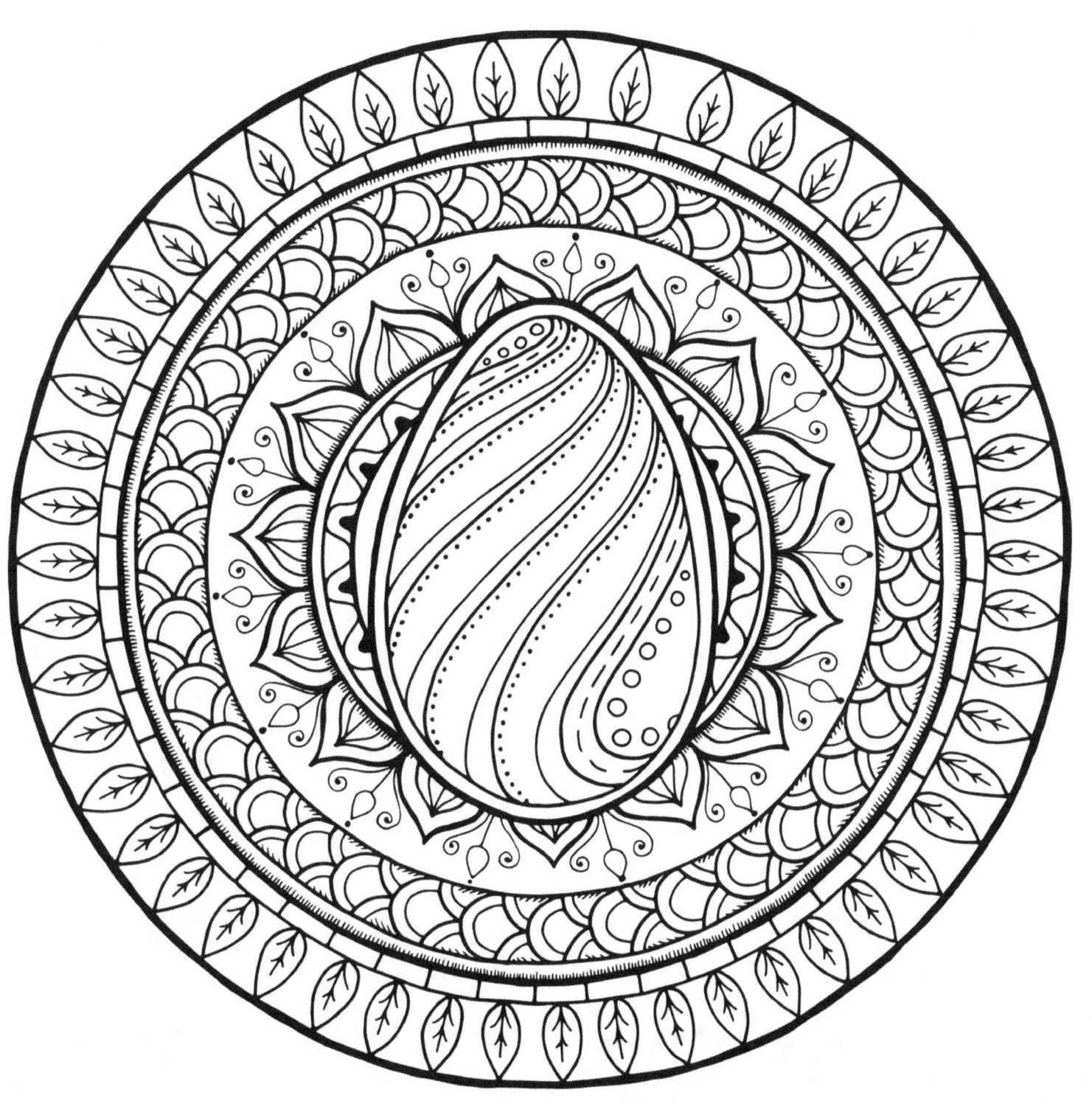

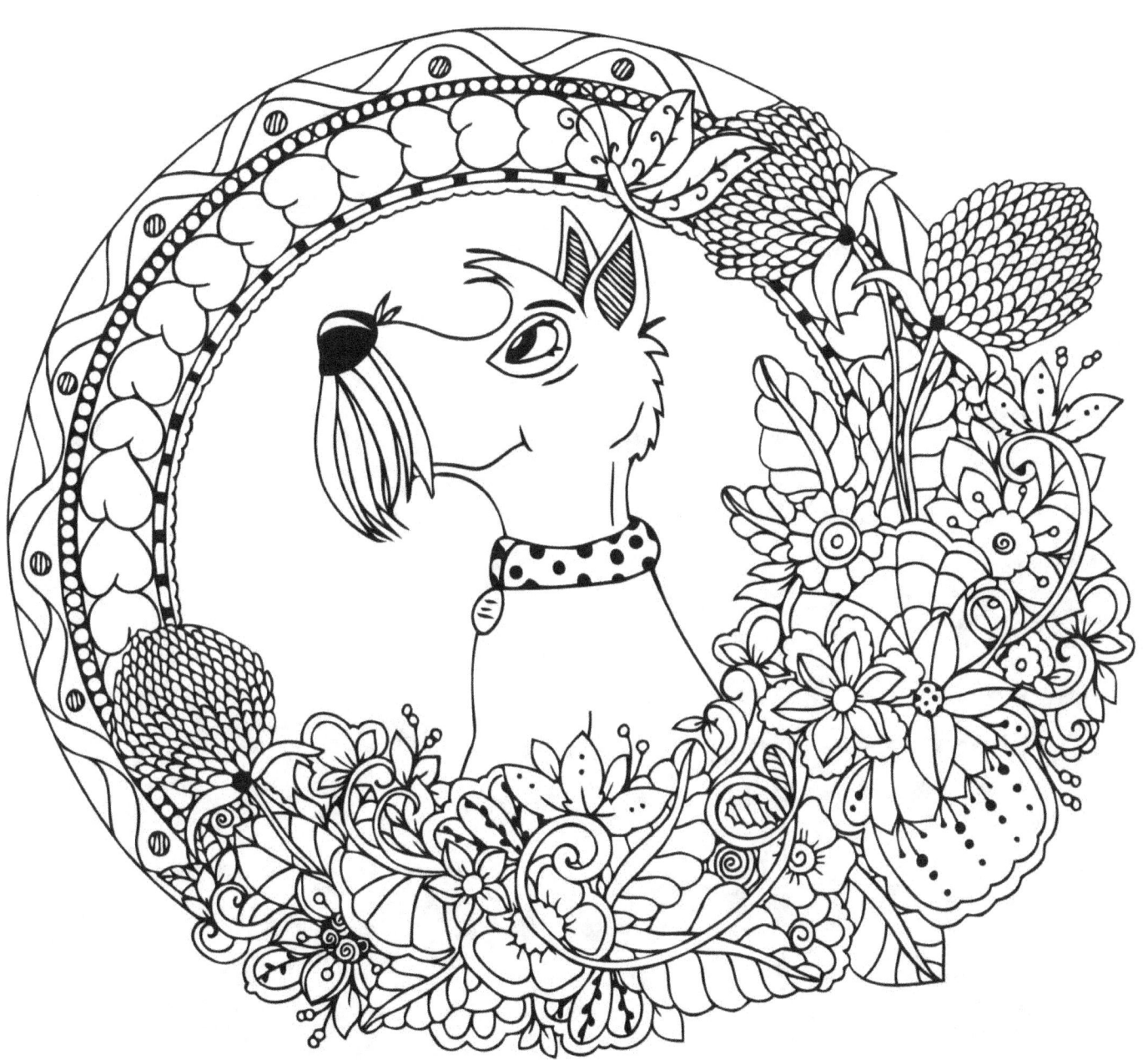

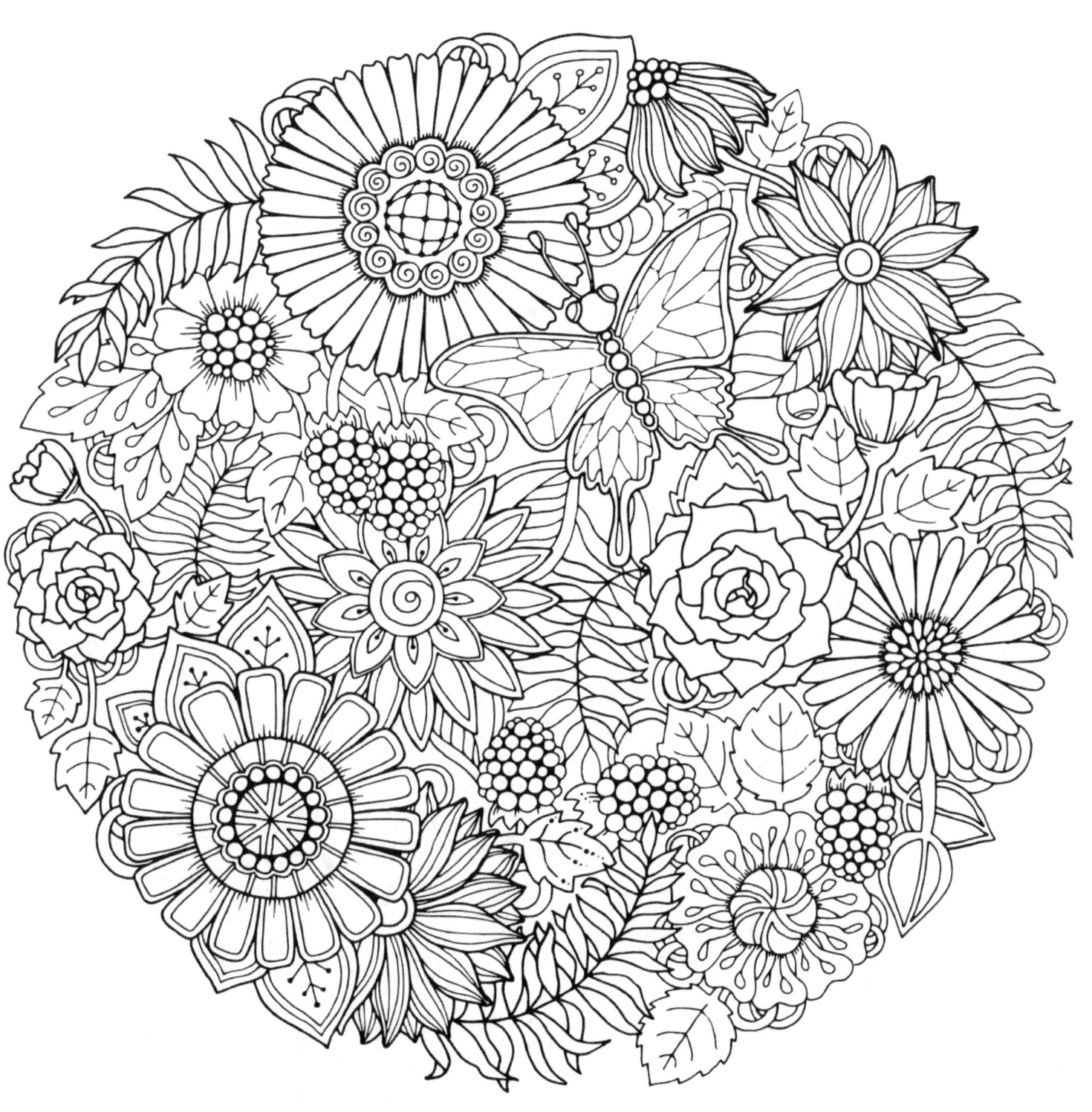

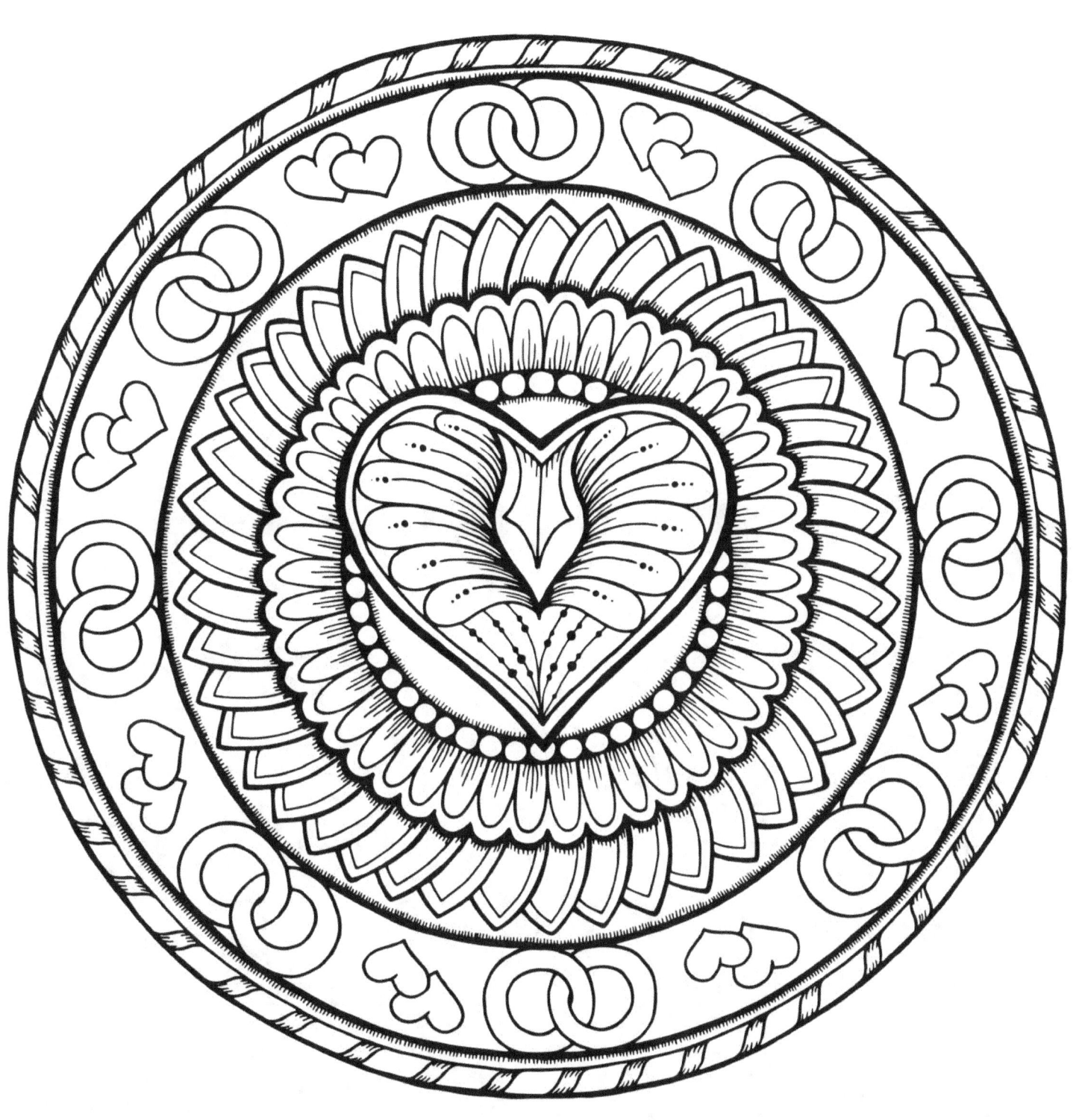

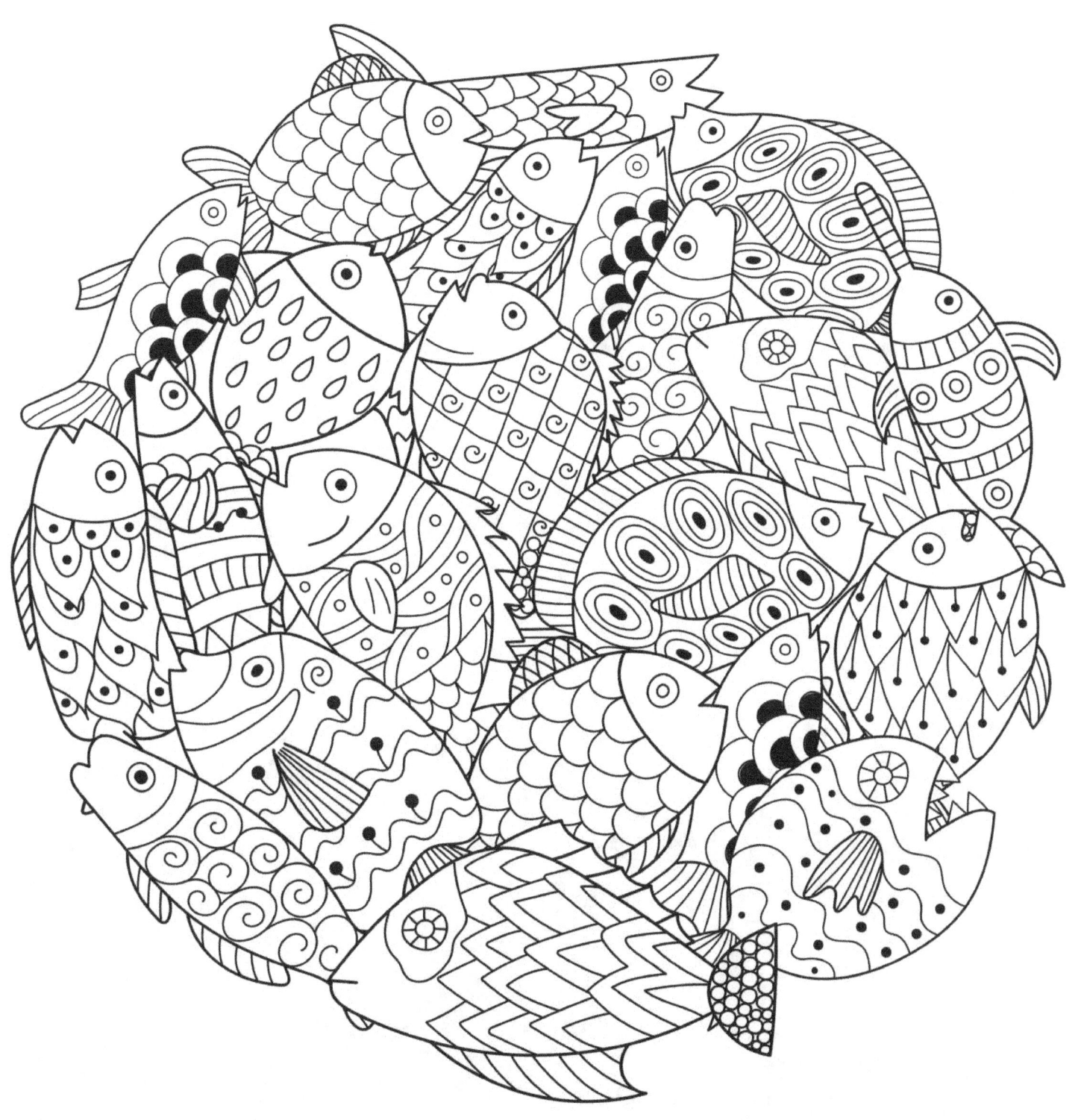

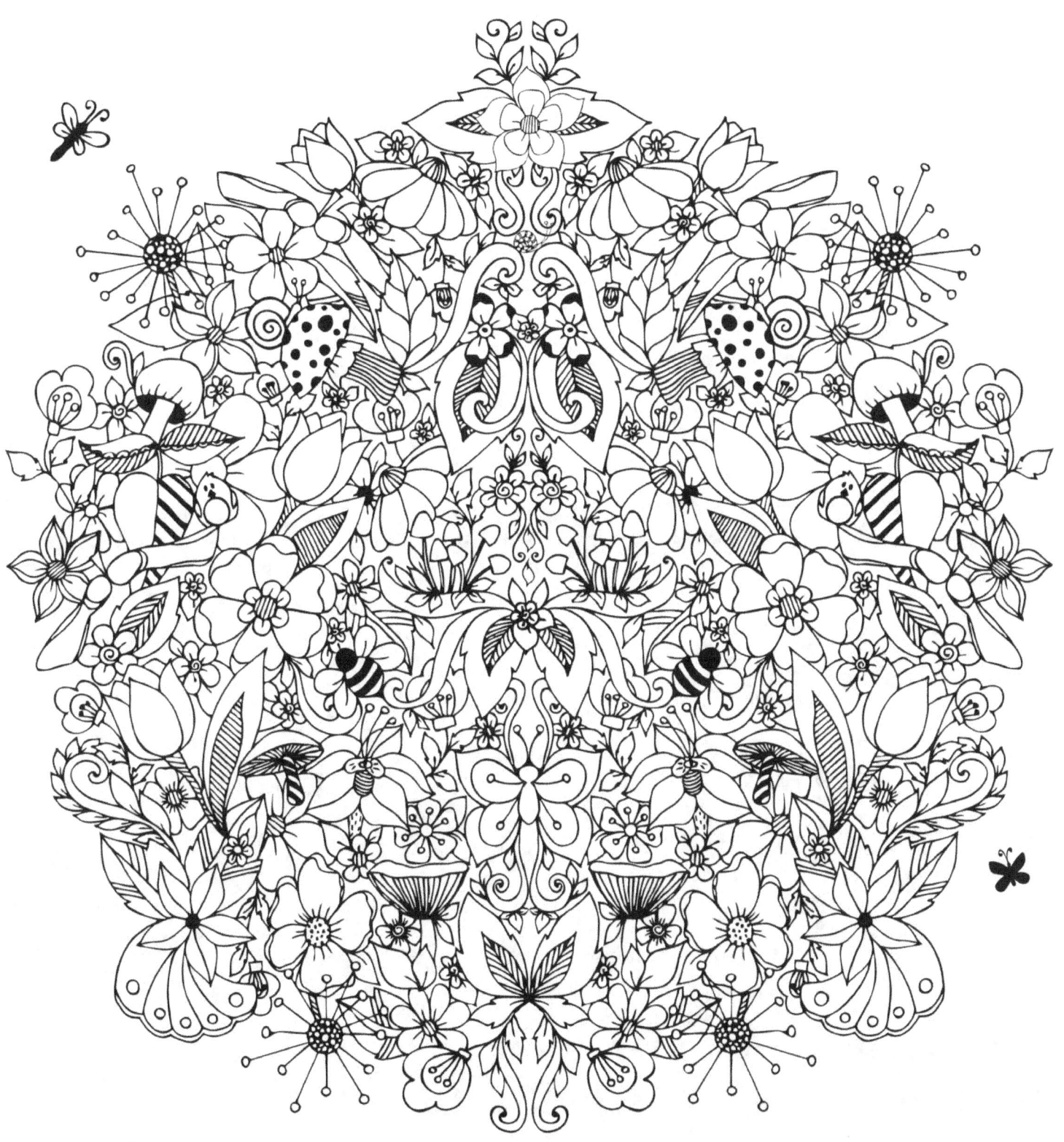

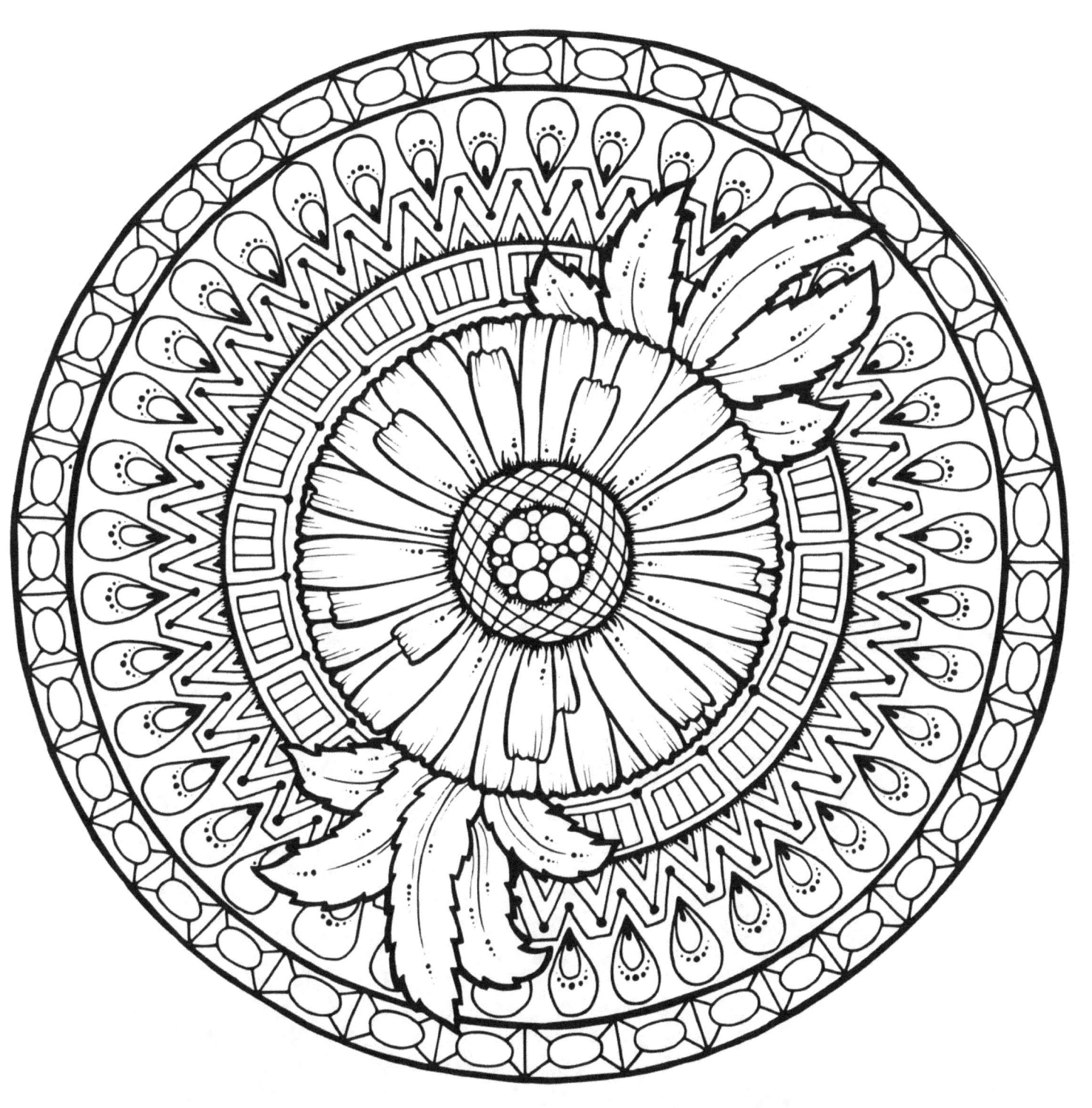

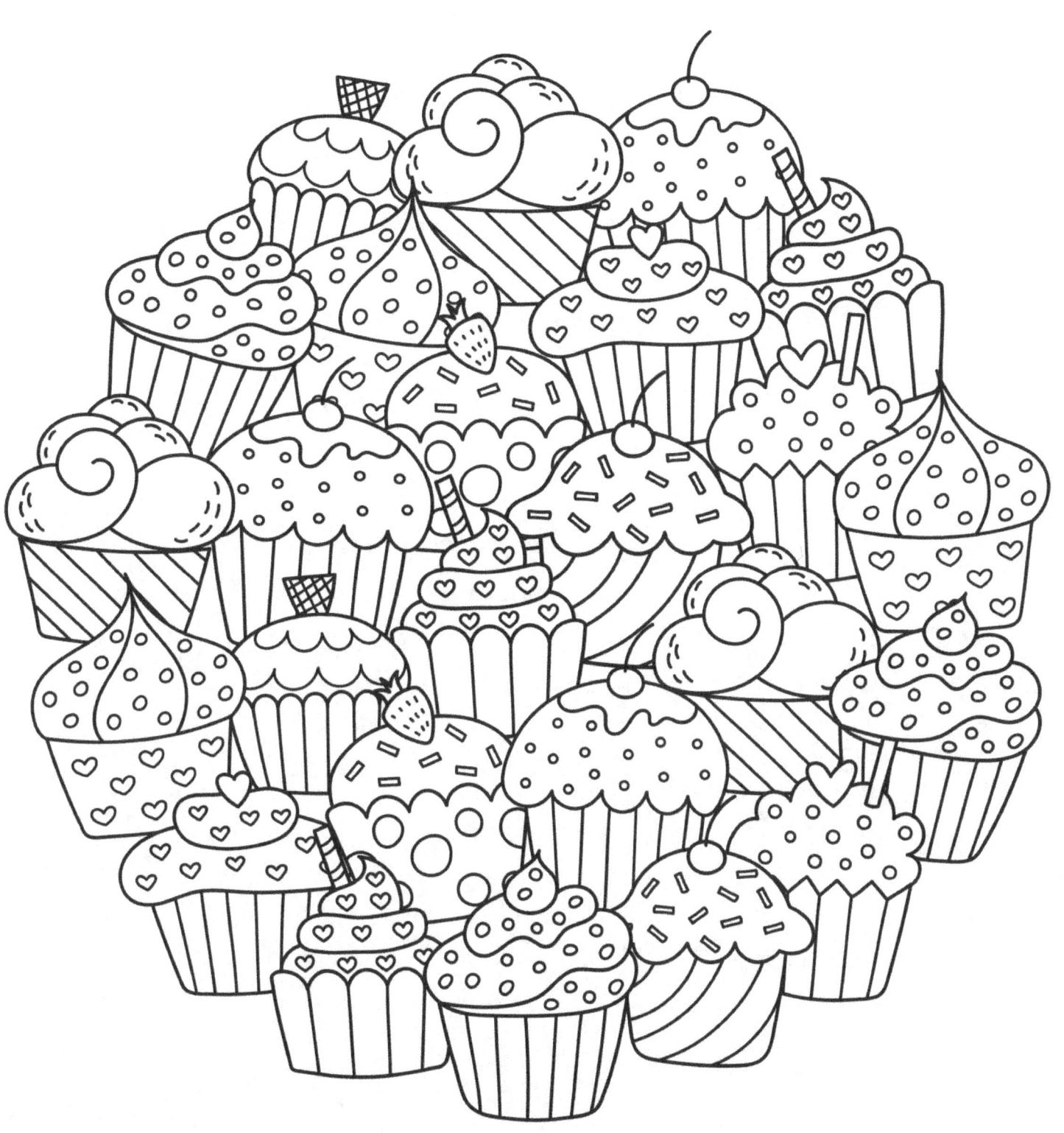

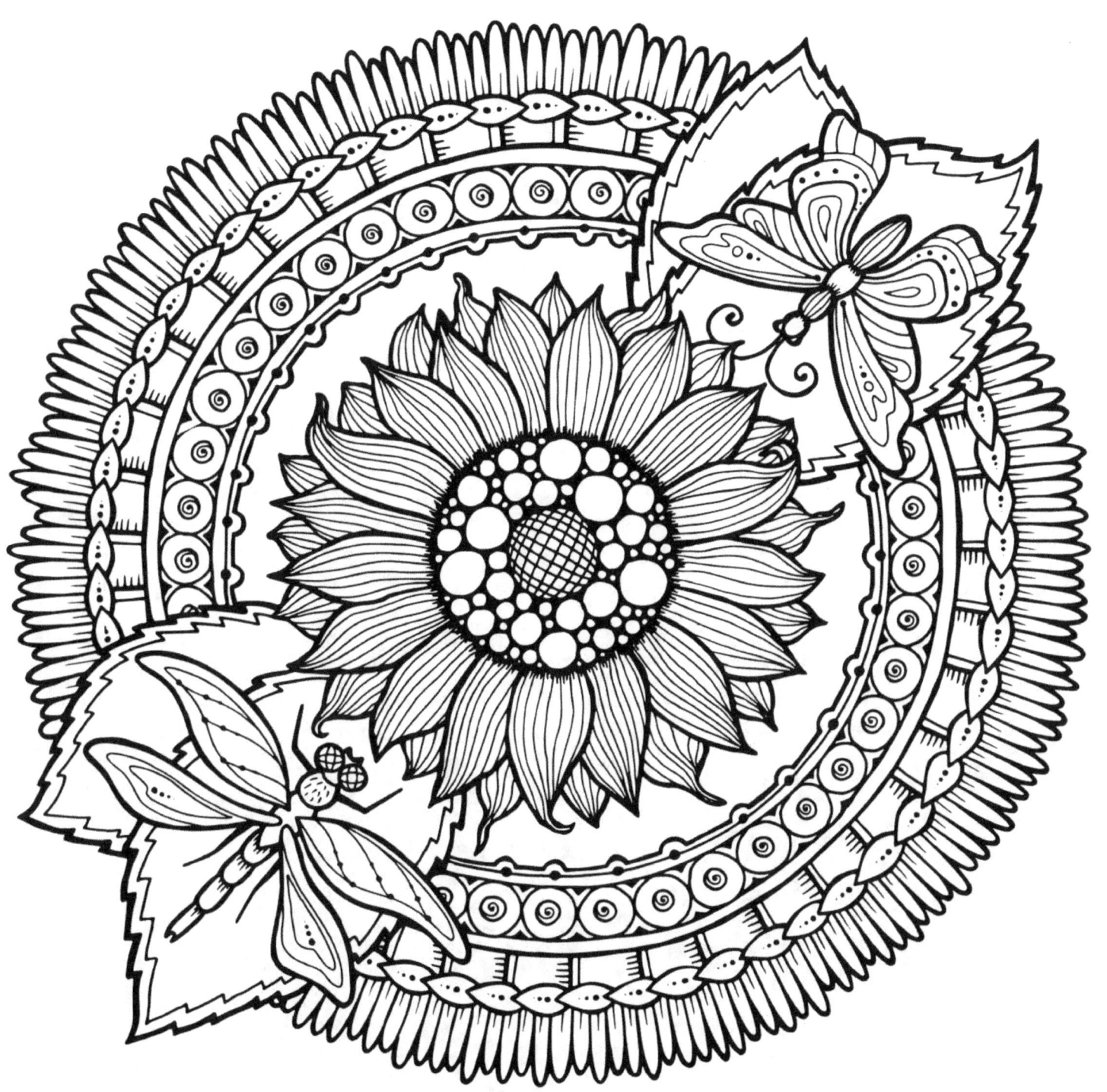

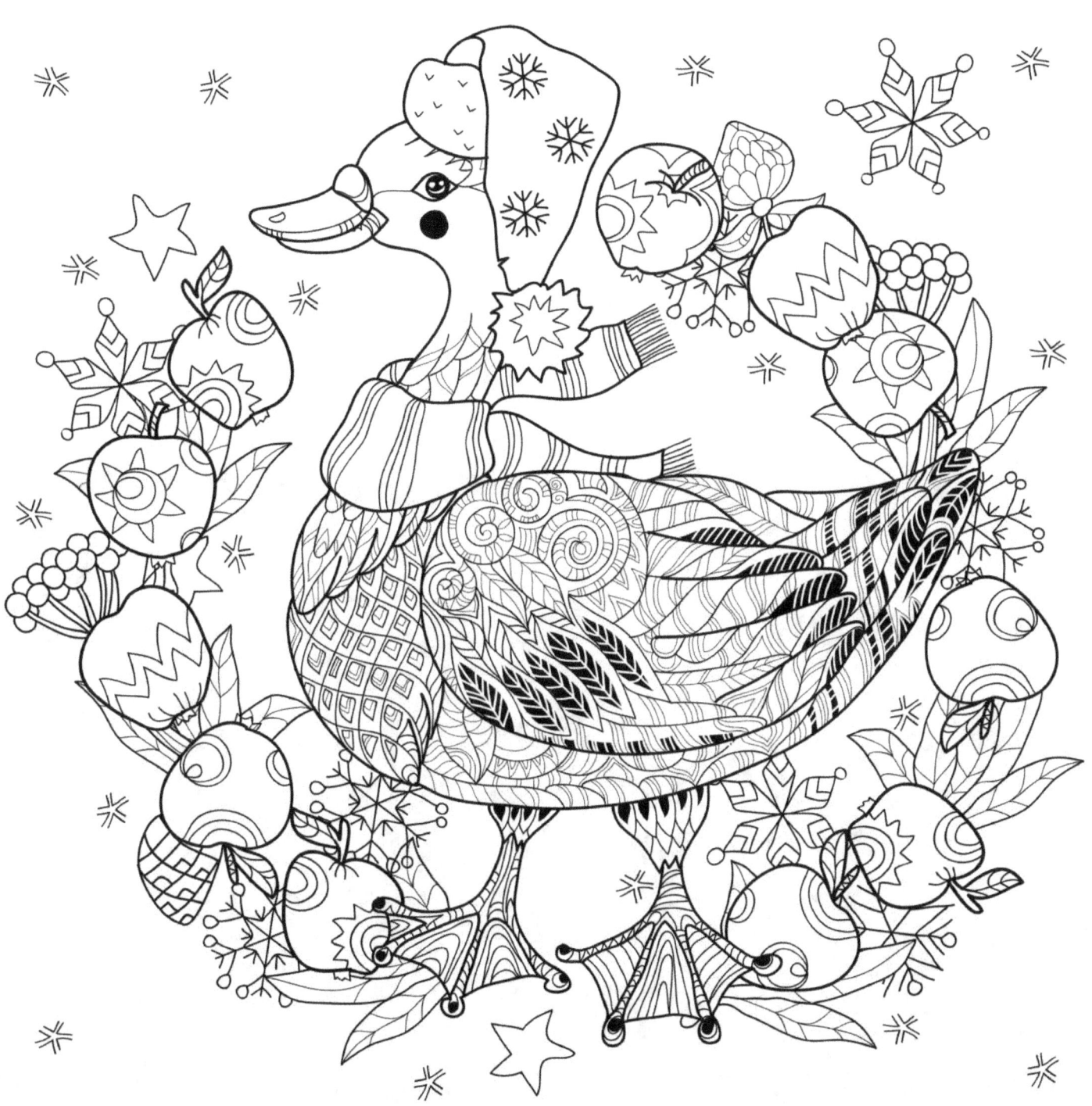

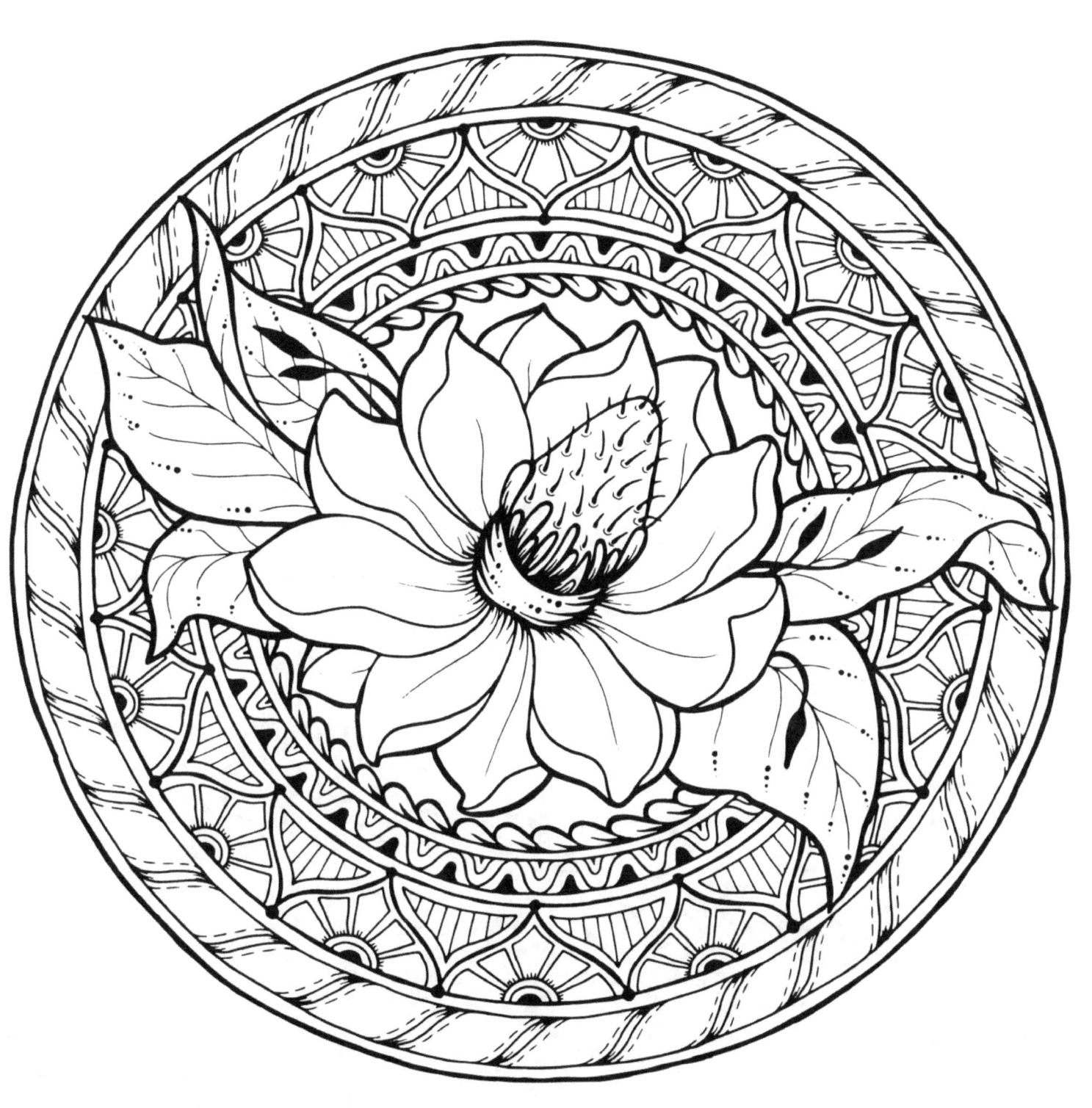

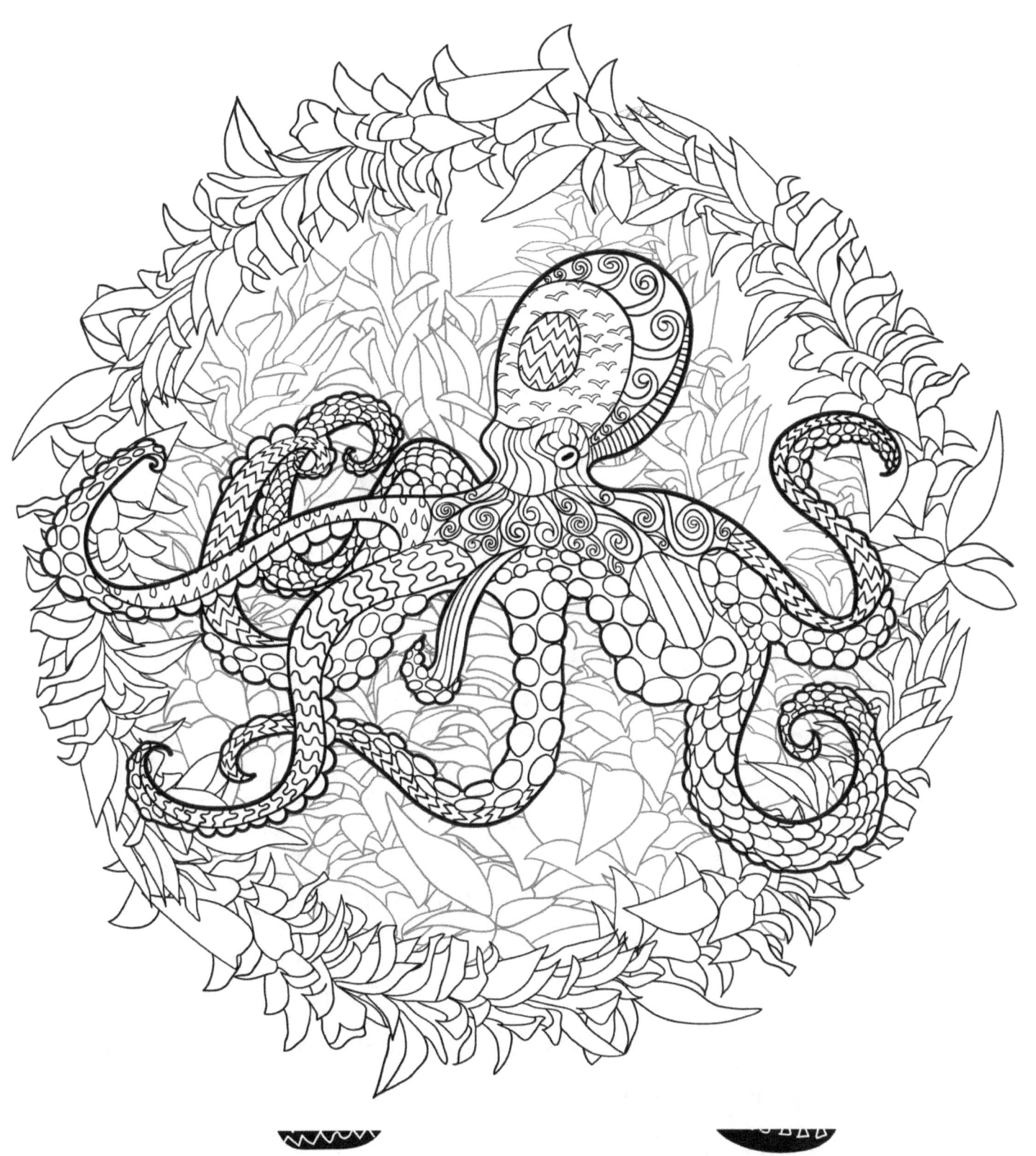

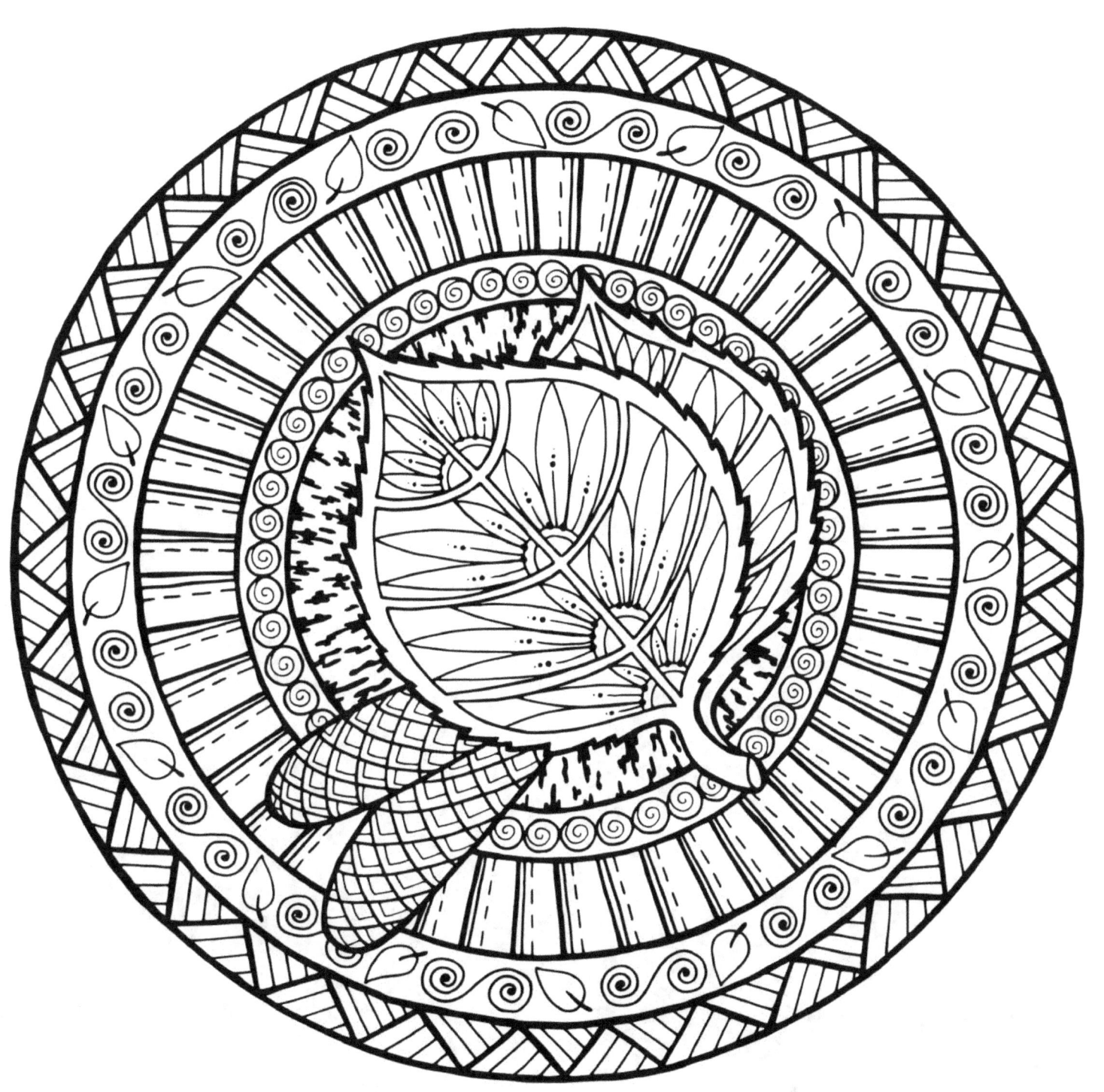

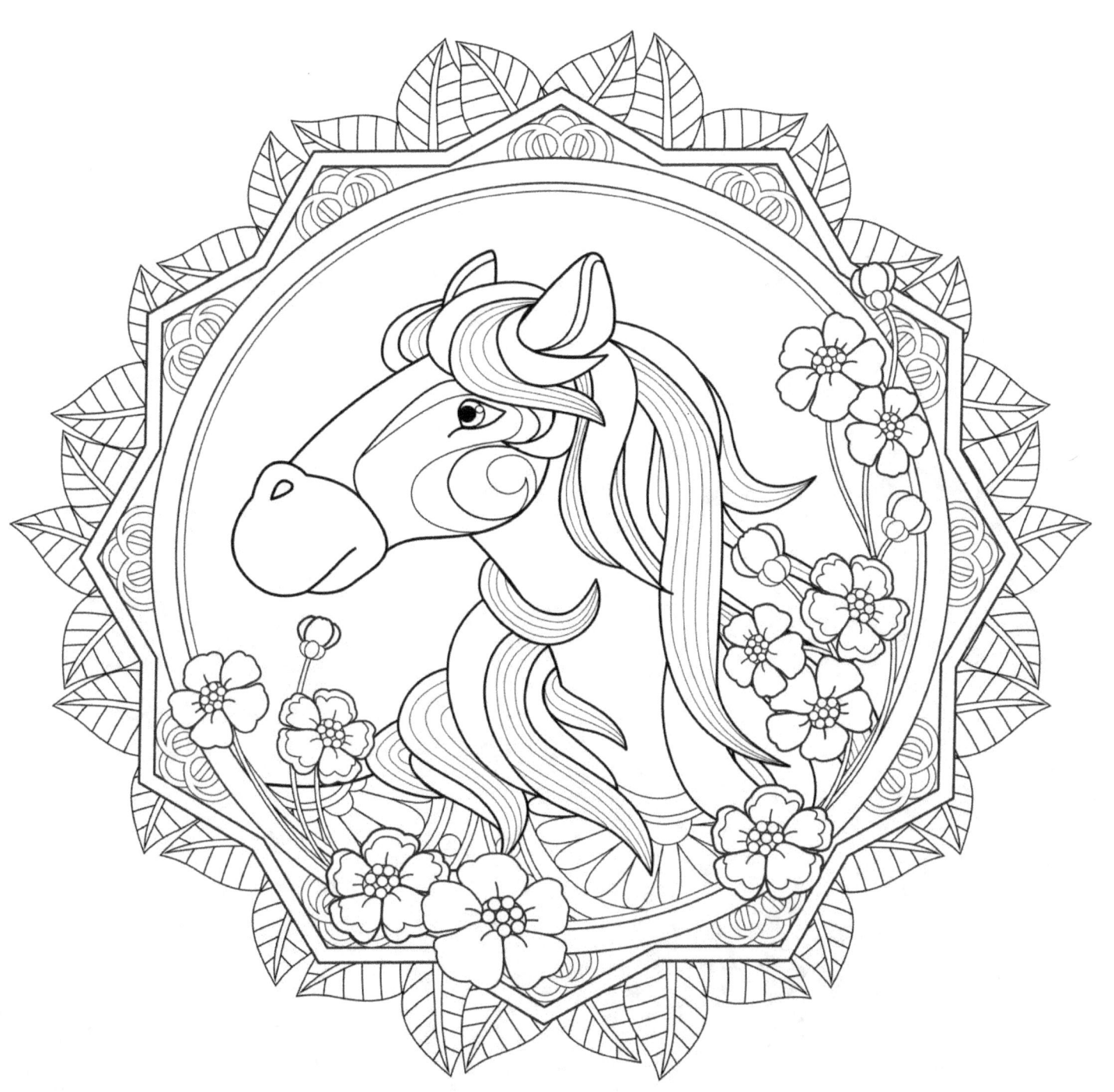

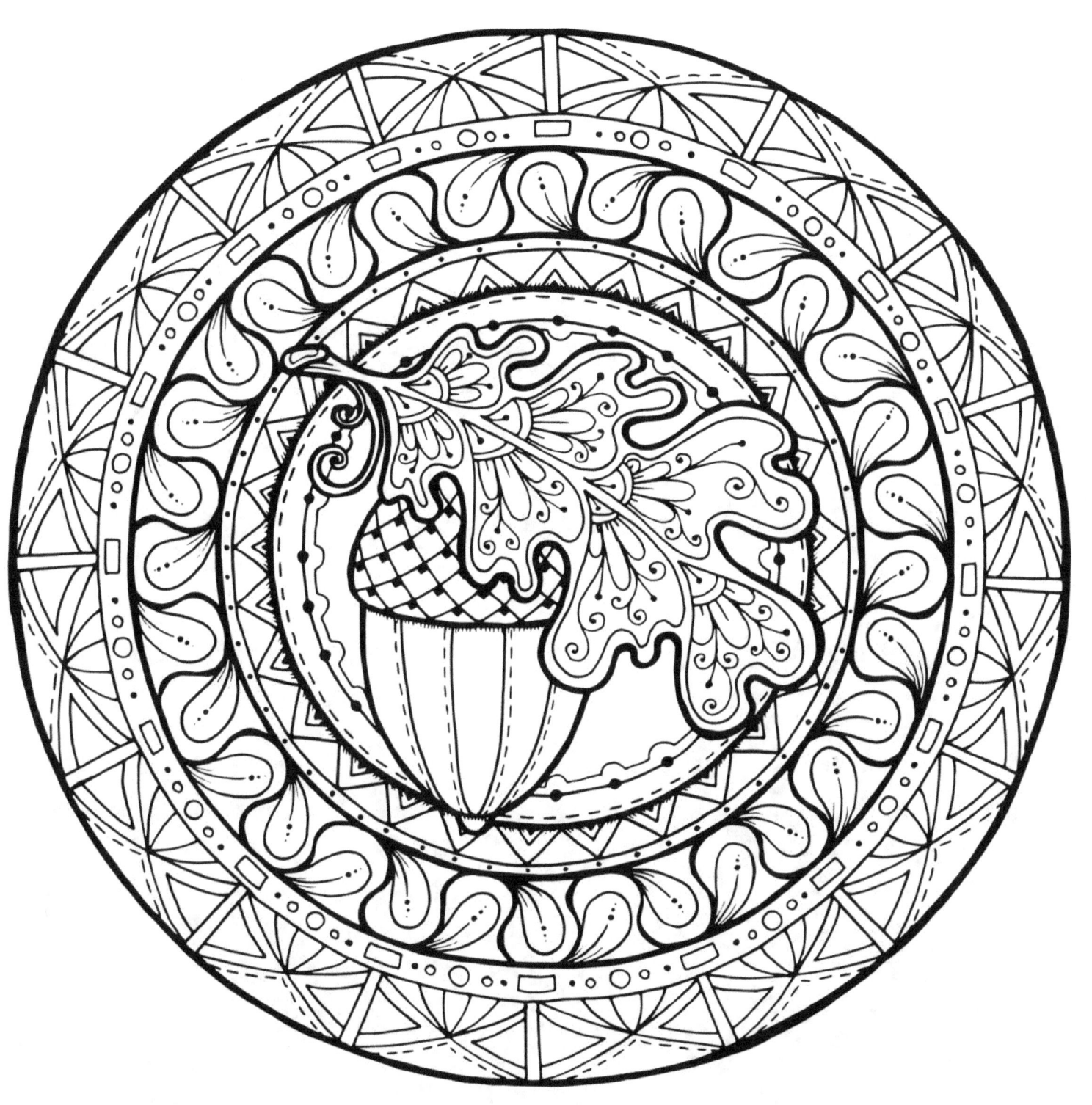

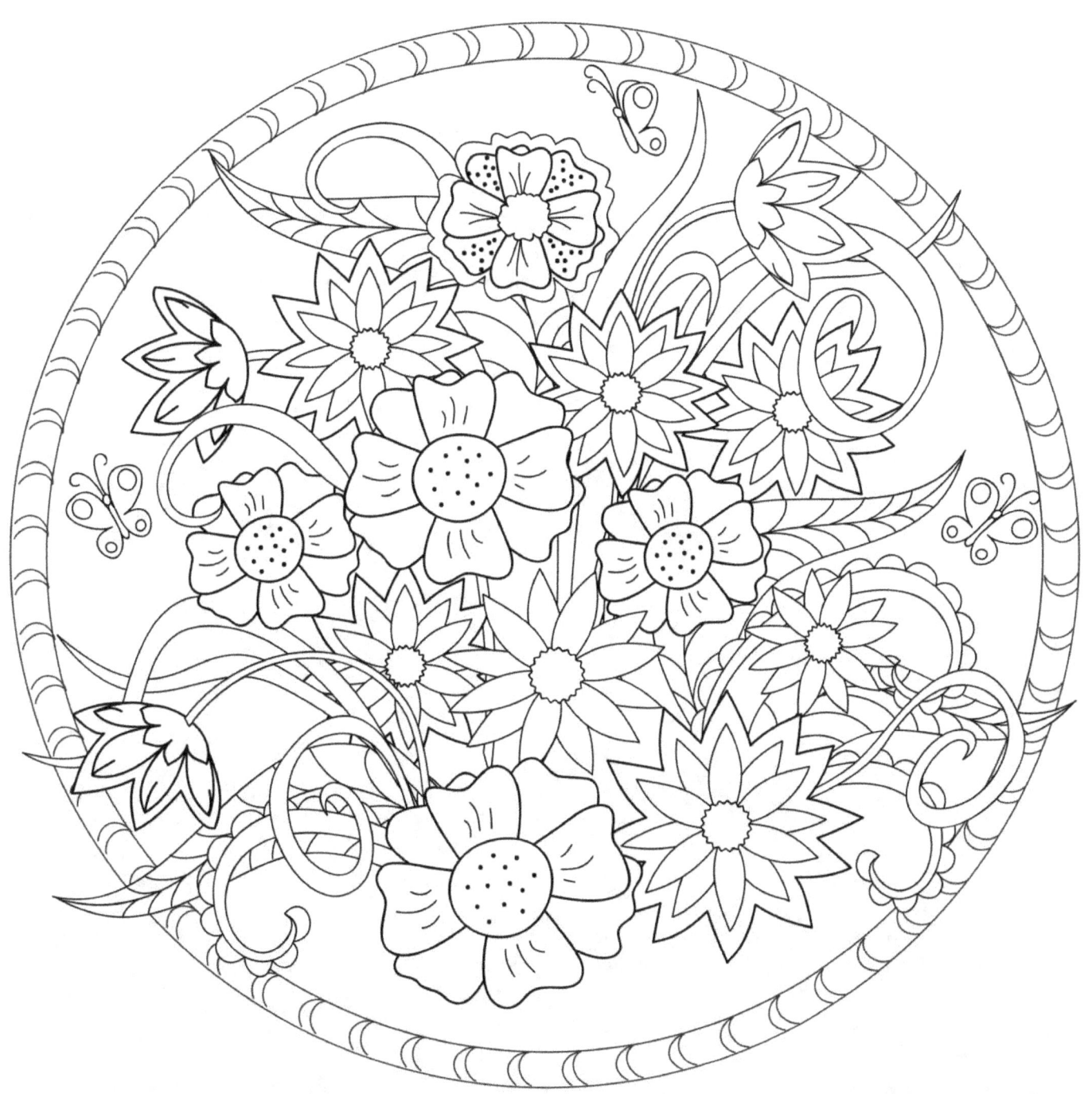

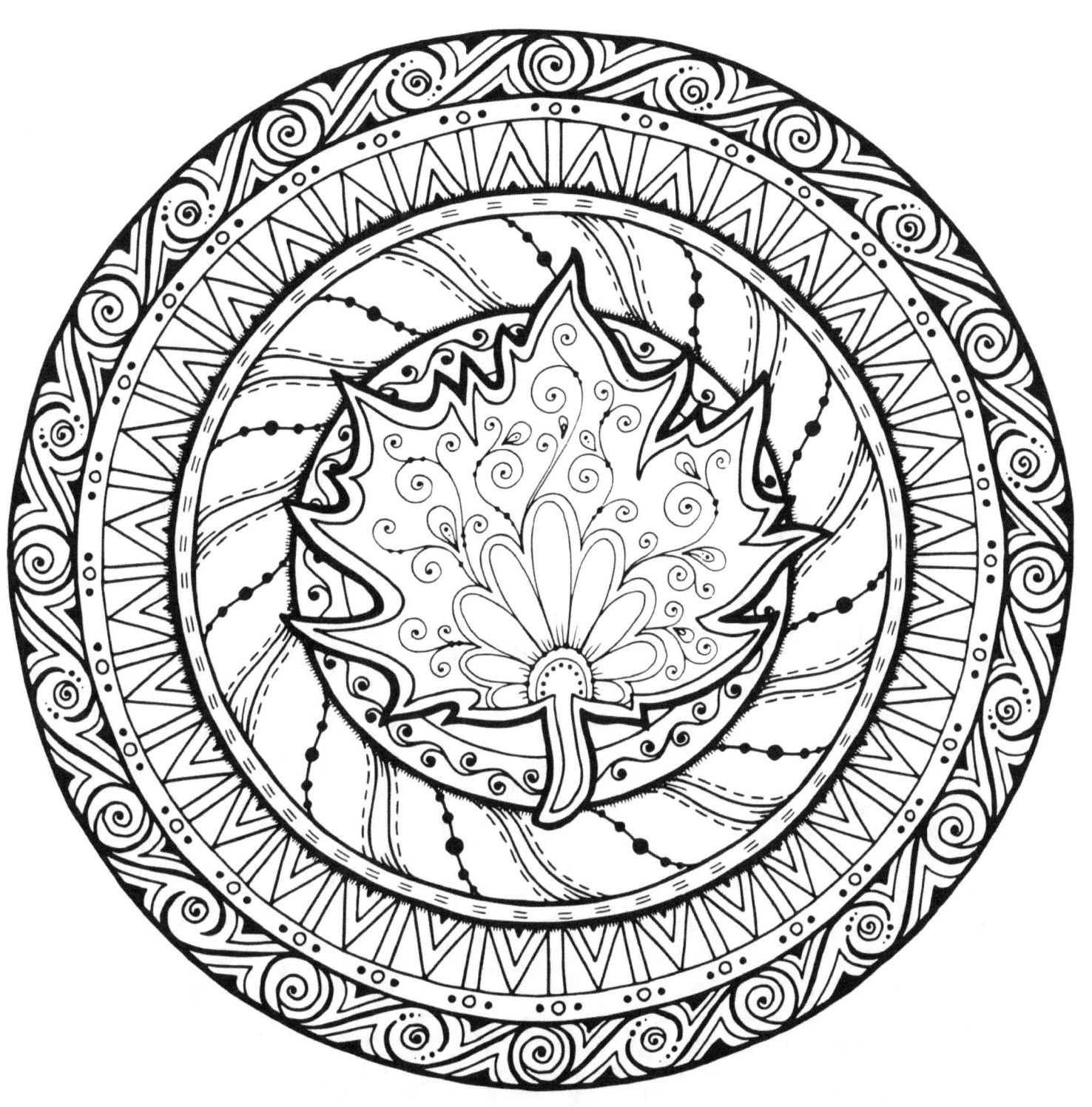

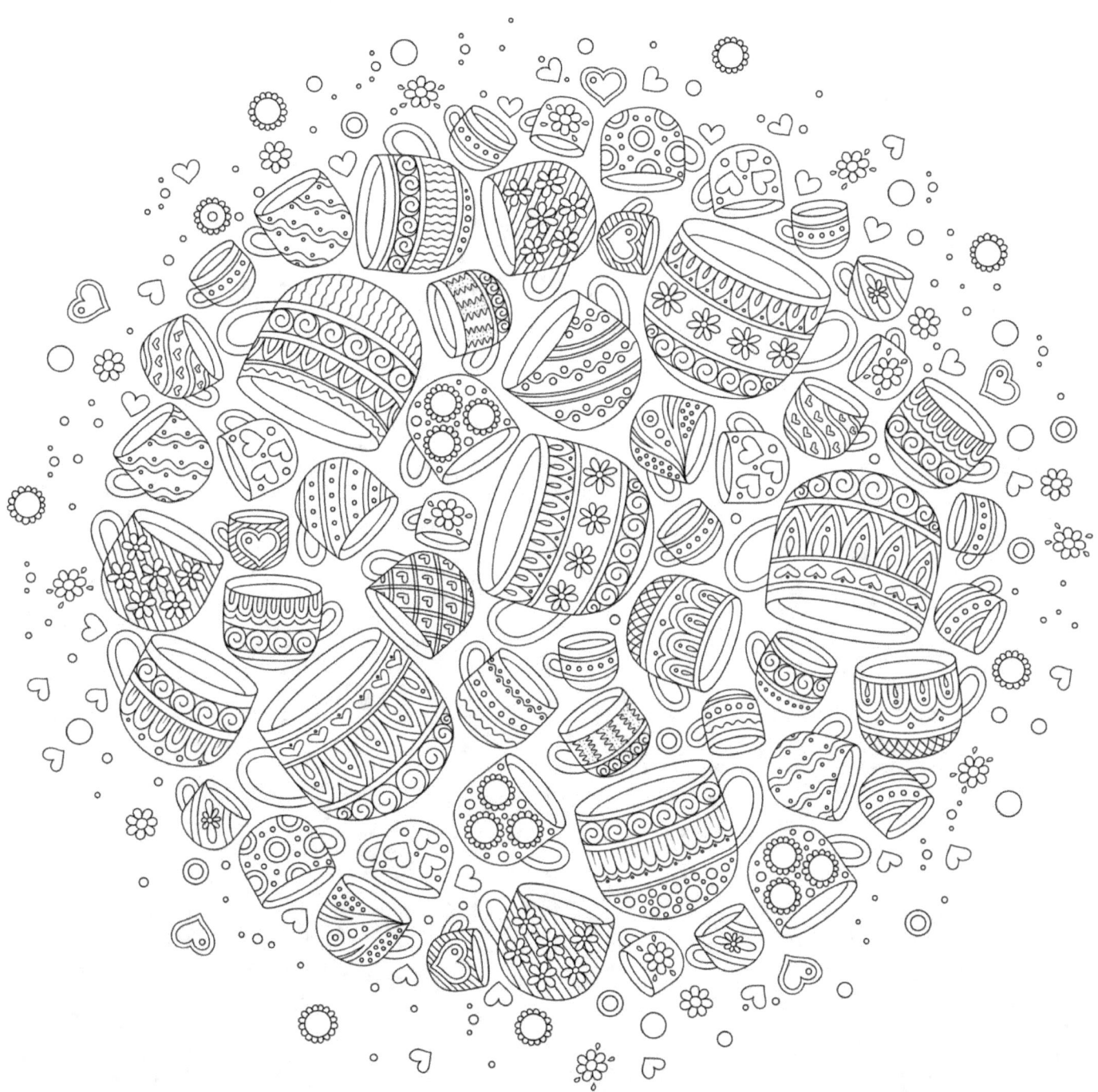

www.ingramcontent.com/pod-product-compliance
Lightning Source LLC
Chambersburg PA
CBHW081900170526
45167CB00007B/3093